In the Sweet Here and Now

In the Sweet Here and Now

A study on the joy of walking with Jesus
on the path of obedience.

Geoffrey E. Garne

Pacific Press Publishing Association
Mountain View, California
Oshawa, Ontario

Cover art by Harry Anderson, artist, © The Church of Jesus Christ of Latter-day Saints. Used by permission.
Cover photos by D. Tank and Joan Walter

Printed in United States of America

Library of Congress Cataloging in Publication Data

Garne, Geoffrey E.
In the sweet here and now.

Bibliography: p.
1. Ten commandments. 2. Spiritual life—
Seventh-day Adventist authors. I. Title.
BV4655.G36 1984 241.5'2 83-13205
ISBN 0-8163-0543-9

To Merri and Peter, David and Maureen,
my children,
who, together with their contemporaries, will,
in the foreseeable future,
be the front line of the
Seventh-day Adventist Church.

Tragedy

To be a slave when one might be a king,
To walk low roads when one might tread the high;
To crawl when one might just as well take wing,
To choose the slime when one might have the sky.

Clarence E. Flynn

In the Sweet Here and Now

Happy are those
  who reject the advice of evil men,
who do not follow the example of
  sinners
or join those who have no use for
  God.
Instead, they find joy in obeying the
  Law of the Lord.

Psalm 1:1, 2, TEV

Contents

Chapter I	13
Chapter II	19
Chapter III	24
Chapter IV	32
Chapter V	43
Chapter VI	50
Chapter VII	62
Chapter VIII	68
Chapter IX	76
Chapter X	92
Chapter XI	98
Chapter XII	103
References	110

Chapter I

My little granddaughter, who is fifteen months old, wears a T-shirt on which are inscribed the words Life Is Delicious.

But, life is far from "delicious" for millions of earth's inhabitants. Many eke out a mere existence in poverty and near starvation. Others live in the shadow of war and under the threat of impending destruction. Unnumbered thousands of others limp through life bereft of health and impaired in body and limb. Others have experienced the heartbreak of having their homes shattered by bereavement or other circumstances. All these would be justified in concluding bitterly that "the more abundant life" is reserved for the favored few and that to them, who suffer under the heel of ill-health, deformity, poverty, tragedy, bereavement, shattered hopes, and thwarted ambitions, the privilege of drawing with joy from "the wells of salvation" (Isaiah 12:3) is something that has been denied.

Yet, in spite of these adverse circumstances, *every* disciple of Jesus may know and experience the joy of the Lord in an intimately personal way *here and now*. The good news of the gospel is that by identifying Himself with the trauma and tragedy, sorrow and suffering of human experience, Jesus Christ made it possible for us to enjoy the peace of heaven in our hearts here and now *in spite of our circumstances*! He took upon Himself the pains of earth so that we might experience the pleasures of heaven. Not just in the sweet bye and bye, but in the sweet here and now!

God intends life to be "delicious" for His people—those who put their trust in Him and claim His sovereignty over their lives.

He gives us many assurances in His Word that He desires this to be the case. In Psalm 16:11 we are told, "Thou wilt shew me THE PATH OF LIFE: in thy presence is fulness of joy; at thy right hand there are pleasures for evermore." Emphasis supplied. As we have mentioned, the prophet Isaiah adds his testimony in chapter 12, verse 3, of his prophecy: "Therefore with joy shall ye draw water out of the wells of salvation." And Jesus declared His purpose for coming to be our Saviour, in John 10:10, when He said, "I am come that they might have life, and that they might have it more abundantly."

"As through Jesus we enter into rest, heaven begins here. We respond to His invitation, Come, learn of Me, and in thus coming we begin the life eternal."—*The Desire of Ages*, p. 331.

The key to this here-and-now happiness, peace, and joy, which transcends circumstance, is a *divine-human relationship*. God made it that way. In the beginning He created man and woman "in his own image." See Genesis 1:26, 27. He made them capable of enjoying His companionship. Adam and Eve found their happiness not merely in the beauty and perfection of their Eden home, but in fellowship and harmony with their God. When they deliberately chose to turn their backs on Him, the relationship was broken. Through sin they severed the link with their source of life and happiness. "Your iniquities have separated between you and your God, and your sins have hid his face from you, that he will not hear." Isaiah 59:2.

The only way the relationship could be restored was by God, in the Person of Christ, throwing Himself across the gap sin had made and closing the circuit sin had broken! From the moment man rebelled against Him, God took the initiative in restoring the fractured relationship. The first picture we have of God after the intrusion of sin is of Him searching for man and calling out to find him. Not that God didn't know where Adam and Eve were hiding. Of course He knew; He knows everything. But He wanted them—*and us*—to know that *He still cared*!

Among the first questions in the Bible is "Where art thou?" (Genesis 3:9)—a question addressed by a searching God to His erring children. And the first question in The New Testament is "Where is he . . .?" (Matthew 2:2)—a question addressed by men seeking their reconciling God. The Old Testament record of man's rebellion opens with the picture of man hiding from God. The New Testament opens with the picture of man following the star to find the way back to God through Christ. Matthew 2:1-10. At the beginning of the Old Testament, man hides away from God in fear. At the beginning of the New Testament, "when they saw the star, they rejoiced with exceeding great joy." Matthew 2:10.

Among the first recorded words of man to God in the Old Testament is the statement, "I was afraid, . . . and I hid myself." Genesis 3:10. How sad! But the reverse side of the coin in the New Testament portrays heavenly heralds delivering to man the message from God, "Fear not. . . . For unto you is born . . . a Saviour, . . . Christ the Lord." Luke 2:10, 11.

This Saviour would "save his people [not in, but] from their *sin*." Matthew 1:21. He would save them from the dominion of sin as well as from the ultimate consequence of transgression—eternal death. See Romans 6:23; Genesis 2:17. And He would deliver them from sin's consequences—bondage to Satan, broken communion with God, destroyed peace, disorientation of life, and all the unhappiness that being out of harmony with God brings.

It stands to reason that if man got himself out of harmony with God by straying from the path of obedience, our Saviour's role would be to restore that harmony by leading us back to the path of obedience! People who suggest that being saved dispenses with the necessity of obedience haven't really looked at the full picture of what salvation is all about. They have failed to take into consideration the first factor of the equation: What is it we need salvation from? The Bible's answer is, sin. The thing that made the plan of salvation necessary was sin—man's sin. The thing that makes salvation possible is grace—God's way of dealing with sin. And what is sin? Transgression. Rebellion. Disobedience. Disharmony with God.

Sin is the problem. God's grace doesn't solve the problem by condoning sin. The moment God did that, He would cease to be a holy God. He saves us by Himself paying the price for our transgression and then restoring us to a relationship of harmony with Him.

It is clear, then, that while we are not saved *by* our obedience, we certainly are not saved *in disobedience*! God saves us *by* grace *through* faith *from dis*obedience *to* obedience!

We certainly are *not* saved *by* obedience! If this were possible, if it were all that is necessary for salvation, then Adam and Eve could have been saved by solemnly promising that they would never again touch the forbidden tree and living up to their promise! Their faithful compliance with that promise would have sufficed for them not to need a Saviour. But because any future obedience, however perfect, could never atone or compensate for past failure, it was necessary for Christ, the second Adam, to stand again on the ground on which Adam had stood; for Him to succeed where Adam had failed; for Him to conquer where Adam had been conquered; for Him to be faithful where Adam had been unfaithful; and for Him to obey where Adam had disobeyed. Only on the basis of Christ's obedience could Adam's disobedience be cancelled out. "Wherefore, as by one man sin entered into the world, and death by sin; and so death passed upon all men, for that all have sinned." "Therefore as by the offence of one judgment came upon all men to condemnation; even so by the righteousness of one the free gift came upon all men unto justification of life. For as by one man's disobedience many were made sinners, so by the obedience of one shall many be made righteous." Romans 5:12, 18, 19.

It is just as certain, on the other hand, that we are not saved *in dis*obedience or *to dis*obedience. If this were possible, all that would have been necessary would have been for God to wink His eye at Adam's transgression and for Him to have swept it under the rug. If God can tolerate and excuse sin in us, then He could also have done so for Adam. The plan of salvation would have been unnecessary. Jesus would not have needed to pay the penalty for man's transgression. God could have solved the sin problem simply by declaring that it didn't really matter and that He was excusing it without any penalty having to be paid. The fact that Christ was required to pay the penalty for man's transgression at such infinite cost should settle it in our minds once and for all that sin just cannot be trifled with and that no command of God, however insignificant it may appear to be, can be violated with impunity.

Indeed it is true that Christ's obedience alone could counterbalance man's disobedience. Our obedience can in no way contribute toward paying the price for our disobedience. Only the merits of Christ's perfect obedience could be accepted as adequate compensation for our transgression. In this sense we can speak of salvation by substitution. The very best we have to offer is utterly inadequate. Only Christ's substitutionary life and death can suffice to pay the penalty for our transgression.

If in speaking of salvation by substitution we mean, however, that since Christ's obedience is all-sufficient, we can carry on sinning to our heart's content, we have really missed the whole point of what salvation is all about! The religious philosophy that says we can carry on sinning because our disobedience or obedience is inconsequential, is by no means new! The founding fathers of the early Christian church had to contend with it in their day, as becomes clear from even casual reading of the epistles of Paul, Peter, John, James and Jude—the full complement of epistolary New Testament writers. Nowhere is the error more forcefully dealt with than by Paul in the sixth chapter of his Epistle to the Romans: "What shall we say then? Shall we continue in sin, that grace may abound? God forbid. How shall we, that are dead to sin, live any longer therein?" "Let not sin therefore reign in your mortal body, that we should obey it in the lusts thereof." "Know ye not, that to whom ye yield yourselves servants to obey, his servants ye are to whom ye obey; whether of sin unto death, or of obedience unto righteousness?" Romans 6:1, 2, 12, 16.

The whole point in this passage of Scripture is that obedience or disobedience is a matter of identifying ourselves with either God or His adversary. And for us to claim to be saved by our Lord and Saviour Jesus Christ while identifying ourselves with His adversary, argues the apostle, is absolutely unthinkable!

In this sense, the term, "salvation by substitution" falls short of presenting the full picture, and it would be more correct to speak of "salvation by identification." It is all-embracing. It includes in the fullest sense the concept of "salvation by substitution," for it acknowledges acceptance of Christ's merits alone as being adequate to pay the penalty of our transgression. But it goes beyond that acceptance to identify ourselves as fully as is humanly possible with His obedience which was rendered perfectly on our behalf.

Such identification will express itself in our Saviour's own identification with His Father's will when He said, "I delight to do thy will, O my God: yea, thy law is within my heart." Psalm 40:8.

Delighting to do God's will because His law is in our hearts, enjoying the keeping of His commandments, finding genuine pleasure in obeying the precepts of His law because in doing so we are identifying ourselves with our Lord and Saviour Jesus Christ—this is what makes it possible for a person, regardless of his circumstances, to declare, "Life is delicious!"

Chapter II

In Australia and, I suppose, some other countries, one can effect a considerable saving in traveling, by flying on what is called standby. Instead of booking one's seat, one waits one's turn until all booked seats have been filled. One time I decided to save the publishing house where I work as an editor some money when I had to fly from Melbourne to Sydney for a one-day meeting. The journey to Sydney went without a hitch. My mission in Sydney completed, I made my way back to the airport, confidently stepped up to the standby desk, and asked for a seat on the next flight to Melbourne.

After tapping on the keys of her computer terminal, the young attendant read her screen and said, "Yes, I have a seat for you." I thanked her and paid her for my ticket. As she handed it to me she said, "Go straight to gate 6. The passengers have already boarded." I dashed up the stairs to gate 6—just as I was told. No sooner had I flopped onto my seat on the plane when the door was shut and the friendly voice of the hostess came over the intercom: "Ladies and gentlemen, welcome on board flight—to Brisbane." Brisbane, of course, is as far from Sydney, due north, as is Melbourne, due south! I bolted from my seat like a bullet and ran up the aisle to where a hostess was standing at the now tightly sealed door. "Lady," I said, "I'm in trouble. I was sent to gate 6, but my destination is Melbourne." Without the slightest sign of panic she picked up her phone and called the terminal. In less than no time, it seemed, the tunnel had been pressed back against the plane and the door opened. After thanking her profusely for her kindness, a very red-faced passenger stepped into the tunnel and rushed to gate 7—the right gate!—and once again, just in time, I collapsed into my seat for my flight home.

The two planes were only a gate apart, but they were heading in opposite directions. The right or the wrong gate spelled the difference between destinations 1200 miles apart.

Serious as it would have been arriving in Brisbane instead of Melbourne, it's peanuts in comparison with what it would be like arriving *out*side instead of *in*side the walls of the City of God when we come to the end of the pilgrim way! The tragedy is that many people who think they are on the flight to the *in*side are going to find out too late that they've landed on the *out*side! Jesus says so in Matthew 7:21-23. These verses must surely contain some of the saddest words in all of the Bible. Notice that Jesus doesn't say "some" or "a few." He says "many." That's sad. They're actually going to expect the gates of the city to swing open to them and are going to be horrified to see them swing closed against them.

These will not be irreligious people—not blasphemers, infidels, criminals. They will say, "Lord, have we not . . . in thy name?" Christ's response to them will be, "I never knew you: depart from me, ye that work iniquity."

There are two things I never want to have happen to me. I don't want to reach my eternal destination and find out too late that I've been on the wrong plane. Even worse, I don't want anybody to come to me in that day and say, "Pastor, I'm lost because you sent me to the wrong gate!" So today I want to help you check your boarding card. What is the formula for salvation? Someone will answer, "We are saved by faith in Christ alone." Correct! We are not saved by faith *plus* works, or even by faith *that* works. We are saved by faith in Christ alone. But faith was never intended to be a substitute for obedience! Faith doesn't make obedience *unnecessary*. Faith makes obedience *possible*! Saving faith will always lead to harmony with God's will. If it doesn't, it is phony!

There are plenty of people around nowadays who have the idea that there are two ways to the kingdom of heaven, and it doesn't matter which of the two you choose. Eventually either will get you to your eternal destination. The one way is the high road of holiness, and the other, the low road of cheap grace. The choice is optional. The high road is desirable, and those who choose it will get a magnificent view of the excellence and glory of God's character. But it is a road that is available to only the favored few, the spiritual elite. For the ordinary traveler, the common sinner, there is the low road. On this route there is no spiritual class distinction. The only qualification is that you "believe in Jesus." The name of Jesus is the magic password that will give anybody access to this road. There are no conditions. No need to change your life. No need to leave anything behind. You can carry on drinking, smoking, cursing, swearing, cheating, stealing, gambling, dancing, even committing adultery. As long as you "accept Jesus," His righteousness will avail, His blood will cover everything, and you'll reach the golden gates just as surely as will those on the other road. In fact, it's possible that on the low road you may even get to the gloryland before them!

The church today is trying to accomodate both groups. It holds before prospective travelers a map on which both routes are depicted. And according to the map held up in its preaching, both routes go through to the kingdom. The high road is warmly recommended. But for those who feel that the high road is a luxury route they cannot afford, there is the alternative route. So do not worry. Use the magic password and leave the rest to "Christ's merits," and you'll get there at last, along with the others!

The Bible, however, offers prospective travelers no such alternatives. As far as God's Word is concerned there is only one road that goes clear through to the kingdom. All other paths of promise peter out in the wilderness of self-delusion. The only other clearly defined road mentioned leads in the opposite direction. Jesus made this abundantly clear in His preaching:

"Enter ye in at the straight gate: for wide is the gate, and broad is the way, that leadeth to destruction, and many there be which go in thereat: because strait is the gate, and narrow is the way, which leadeth unto life, and few there be that find it." Matthew 7:13, 14. Cf. Luke 13:24.

There is only one way to heaven, not two. The road, the only road, that goes through to the kingdom is the high road—the high road of holiness. And, make no mistake, the password by which one gains access to *that* road *is the name of Jesus*! "Neither is there salvation in any other: for there is none other name under heaven given among men, whereby we must be saved." Acts 4:12. Jesus said, "I am the way . . . : no man cometh unto the Father, BUT BY ME." John 14:6. Emphasis supplied.

But the heaven-bound road to which Jesus introduces us, onto which He invites us, on which He accompanies us, is never a road on which we are made to feel comfortable with our sins! If you suppose you are on the way to heaven and are comfortable with your sins, please take warning that you're on the wrong plane!

The surest way you can know you're on the wrong plane is if you are comfortable with your sins—trying to accomodate them, trying to carry them along with you and hoping against hope that you'll be able to keep them with you clear through to the end of the way. And all the while, you even imagine you can see the smile of Jesus resting approvingly upon you and that His gentle, compassionate smile is saying to you, "Never mind. I know you're only human. I know you can't really help sinning. So carry on. My righteousness will make up for your unrighteousness. It doesn't really matter if you keep on sinning. I'll make up the difference." The name of this plane is self-deception. It seems right, but it leads to death. See Proverbs 14:12; 16:25.

Conversely, the surest way you can know that you're on the flight that leads home, the Jesus Way, is if you're uncomfortable with your sins! You may not be able to claim to be sinless. Far from it. But you're not comfortable with sin. You're not trying to accomodate it. You're not making a studied effort to carry it along with you. On the contrary you're wanting to get rid of it, to shed it as fast as you can. If the "Jesus" who is accompanying you doesn't make you uncomfortable with sin, friend, beware! It isn't the real Jesus. It's a false christ, an antichrist, a demon transformed into an angel of light! Don't be deceived! Jesus, the real Jesus, never saves us *in* our sins or *with* our sins, but *from* our sins. "Thou shalt call his name JESUS [Hebrew, Joshua, meaning Deliverer]: for he shall save his people from their sins." Matthew 1:21.

Jesus came not only to save us from the penalty of past sins and from the presence of sin in the glorious future, but to break the POWER of SIN in our lives here and now.

The fact is that both extremes are to be avoided, the one that leads down into the thicket of self-deception and the one that leads up onto the cliffs of despair. In between the two lies the real road, the only road that leads home. It is the road that bears this sign:

1. Salvation Is Salvation From Sin.
2. Salvation Which Does Not Save From Sin Is No Salvation at All.
3. Jesus Came to Make My Salvation Possible.
4. Jesus Came to Save Me From My Sins, Not in My Sins or With My Sins.
5. He is able to Save "to the Uttermost." That Is, Completely.
6. Because of What He Has Done, Is Doing, and Will Continue to Do for My Salvation, Victory, Complete Victory Over Sin, Is Possible for Me!
7. Therefore in the Light of the Provisions of His Full Salvation, and Accompanied by Him, the Pursuit of Holiness Is a Joyous Experience!

Chapter III

The Ten Commandments are a statement of normalcy. They spell out the elements of a normal relationship between man and God, between man and his fellowman, and between a man and his inner self. Any deviation from the principles outlined in this manifesto of relationships constitutes *ab*normality, a breach of relationships, a departure from the normal human experience God intended man to enjoy.

The whole of God's law is involved with relationships—our relationships with God and man. The law opens with the words "the Lord thy God," closes with "thy neighbour," and in the middle is the word "thou." It thus introduces me to a relationship with God on the one hand, and with my neighbor on the other. It places me as the pier in the bridge between God and my neighbor.

The expression most commonly used in Scripture to describe the normal relationship between man and God is the now-old-fashioned word *walking*. Picture in your mind the fellowship and communion enjoyed in Bible times by two people walking together—not from the house to the garage, but from town to town! In some cultures this privilege is still enjoyed, as in parts of Africa, where I spent most of my life. (Or should I say it is enjoyed in those parts of Africa which are still unspoiled by the mechanized motion of so-called civilization!) Here our Christian believers will walk for not hours but days, to attend camp meeting! I can only imagine the unforgetable association they enjoy as they walk along together over hill and dale. For as they walk, they never stop talking! And laughing! And singing! To them, you see, walking is communication. It kind of gives a fresh slant on what the Bible means when it says, "Enoch walked with God," doesn't it?

The Bible has an amazing lot to say about walking. Yes, "Enoch walked with God." Genesis 5:24. Abraham and Isaac *walked* before God. Genesis 24:40; 48:15. God said of David that he *walked* before Him. 1 Kings 9:4. The Psalms open with a blessing on the man who "*walks* not in the counsel of the ungodly." Psalm 1:1. Paul admonishes those who bury their old lives in the waters of baptism, that they should *walk* "in newness of life." Romans 6:4. He says that Christ's followers "*walk* not after the flesh, but after the Spirit." Romans 8:4. Furthermore we should *walk* in good works; *walk* worthy of our calling; *walk* circumspectly, (see Ephesians 2:10; 4:1; 5:15); *walk* worthy of the Lord (see Colossians 1:10; 1 Thessalonians 2:12); *walk* honestly (see 1 Thessalonians 4:12). "As you have received Christ," he appeals, "so *walk* . . . in him." Colossians 2:6.

John takes up the same strain. "If we *walk* in the light, as he is in the light, we have fellowship one with another, and the blood of Jesus Christ his Son cleanseth us from all sin." "He that saith he abideth in him ought himself also so to *walk*, even as he *walked*." 1 John 1:7; 2:6.

What does walking with Jesus involve? The Bible gives us some clear answers. "This is love, that we *walk* after his commandments. This is the commandment, That, as ye have heard from the beginning, ye should *walk* in it." 2 John 6.

This truth is emphasized repeatedly in the Bible. When God brought His people out of Egypt, He sent manna from heaven on six days but not on the Sabbath to "prove them, whether they will *walk* in my law, or no." Exodus 16:4. Cf. verses 27-30. He promised them that if they would *walk* in His statutes and keep His commandments He would *walk* among them and be their God, and they would be His people. See Leviticus 26:3, 12. Joshua appealed to them "to love the Lord your God, and to *walk* in all his ways, and to keep his commandments, and to cleave unto him, and to serve him with all your heart and with all your soul." Joshua 22:5. We have here a meaningful sequence of verbs: *love*, *walk*, *keep*, *cleave*, and *serve*. In Ezekiel 36:26, 27, God promises us that when He gives us "a new heart" and puts His spirit within us, we will *walk* in His statutes and *keep* His judgments and do them.

Yes, being a Christian is *not all talk*. It's *walk*! And God wants us to *enjoy* that *walk!*

Walking with Jesus is a love relationship with Him. "Can two walk together, except they be agreed?" Amos 3:3. Walking together involves walking in the same direction. Walking with Jesus means that we will love the things He loves and hate the things He hates. The Living Bible renders Amos 3:3, "How can we walk together with your sins between us?" Sin brings separation. (See Isaiah 59:2.) We must "give up all that would separate us from Him."—*Steps to Christ*, p. 44. If we want to walk with Jesus we must renounce sin. This does not mean that we have to reach the point of sinless perfection before we can walk with Jesus, for it is only by walking with Jesus that we can ever reach the point of sinless perfection! But it does mean that our attitude toward sin will be one of distaste.

A love relationship with Jesus is a *loving-obedience relationship*. The keeping of the commandments does not, however, lead us into a relationship with Jesus; a relationship with Jesus leads us into the keeping of His commandments!

The Elements of Normalcy

Notice how these ten eternal precepts reach out, like ten searching fingers, to touch every part of my being:

The first two commandments touch my religious life, my life of worship, my inner life. They break down the idols, the false gods in my heart, and then enthrone God as King of kings and Lord of lords, exclusively supreme.

The third commandment touches my tongue, my words, my speech.

The fourth commandment touches my time. It affects my physical, spiritual, social, and intellectual well-being by directing me to devote time to things eternal as well as to the things that are temporal.

The fifth commandment touches my home. It deals with my family relationships.

The sixth commandment touches my attitude toward the dignity of human life.

The seventh commandment touches my social life, with specific reference to sex.

The eighth commandment touches my business dealings.

The ninth commandment touches my communications.

The tenth commandment touches my motives.

In His law, the supremacy of God is revealed. He declares Himself to be God over all. Notice how forcibly this is revealed:

1. I am God over all gods
2. I am God over all things
3. I am God over all names
4. I am God of time and eternity; I am the God of Creation
5. I am God of the home
6. I am the God of life
7. I am the God of marriage
8. I am the God of property and possessions
9. I am the God of truth
10. I am the God who searches the hidden secrets of the heart

The law of God teaches us how we are to worship God. If the precepts of the Ten Commandments were to be stated positively, they could read something like this:

1. Worship the Lord your God exclusively
2. Worship the Lord your God spiritually
3. Worship the Lord your God reverently
4. Worship the Lord your God as He wills to be worshiped
5. Worship the Lord your God with a humble heart
6. Worship the Lord your God with a kind heart
7. Worship the Lord your God with a pure heart
8. Worship the Lord your God with an honest heart
9. Worship the Lord your God with a truthful heart
10. Worship the Lord your God with an unselfish heart

Notice *how completely* the Ten Commandments reveal my duty to God and to my neighbor. The first four commandments, which reveal my duty to God, teach me to respect:

1. The supremacy of God
2. The spiritual nature of God
3. The holy name of God

4. The sovereign authority of God

The last six, which reveal my duty to my neighbor, teach me to respect:

5. The authority of my parents
6. The life of my neighbor
7. The home and marriage of my neighbor
8. The property of my neighbor
9. The integrity of my neighbor's reputation and character
10. With my mental attitude my neighbor and all that is my neighbor's

The commandments of God furthermore reveal His claim over every faculty of my being:

1. and 2. My heart and soul and spirit; my emotions, my affections, my worship, my allegiance
3. My tongue, lips, and voice
4. My time
5. My home
6. My life
7. My body
8. My property
9. My human relationships
10. My thoughts and feelings

Nothing escapes His sovereignty. He made all. He owns all. He rules all. He claims all. He is King over all. All this is revealed to us in His wonderful law.

Every sin that exists in the world is revealed and condemned by the law of God. No species of evil escapes its all-embracing reach. It lays bare the sins of society, the sins of the body, the sins of the tongue, the sins of the mind, the sins of the spirit. These would be included:

1. The sin of arrogance and pride
2. The sin of materialism
3. The sin of blasphemy
4. The sin of disloyalty and anarchy
5. The sin of disrespect
6. The sin of hatred
7. The sin of lust
8. The sin of dishonesty

9. The sin of untruthfulness
10. The sin of selfishness

Obedience to God's law sets a man free from these vile evils. That is what David meant when he wrote in Psalm 19:7, "The law of the Lord is perfect, converting the soul." Their precepts teach him and build these qualities into his character:

1. Humility and sincerity
2. Spirituality
3. Reverence
4. Loyalty
5. Respect
6. Love
7. Purity
8. Honesty
9. Truthfulness
10. Unselfishness

These are the traits that are going to fit us for eternity. That is why God promises to write His law in the hearts of those who are preparing to meet Jesus in peace when He comes. Read Jeremiah 31:33; Ezekiel 36:26, 27; and Hebrews 8:10. Notice that in these promises God says of those who thus allow Him to write His law in their hearts, that He will be their God and they will be His people. This work of grace whereby God writes His law in the hearts of His people is a work of the Holy Spirit in the life, whereby the principles of God's law become the in-wrought way of life of the new-covenant Christian. When God's law is thus written on the tables of our hearts, it no longer reads "thou shalt" and "thou shalt not." Because His Spirit has written it within my soul, it now reads this way:

1. I will have no other gods before Him
2. I will not bow down to graven images
3. I will hold the name of the Lord my God in reverence
4. I will remember to keep holy the Sabbath of the Lord my God
5. I will honor my father and my mother
6. I will respect my fellow human's right to life
7. I will be pure in my social relationships
8. I will be honest in all my dealings

9. I will be truthful in all my communications
10. I will be content with what God has given me

Like lights that shine brightest when the night is darkest, God will have a people at the end of time who will stand out in dazzling contrast to the gross darkness that surrounds them, distinguished by the fact that they are a people who are:

1. Worshipers of the true God
2. A spiritual people
3. A reverent people
4. A people who are loyal to God's authority
5. A people who are characterized by their family life
6. A loving, gentle people
7. A pure people
8. An honest people
9. A truthful people
10. An unselfish people

"If we abide in Christ, if the love of God dwells in us, our feelings, our thoughts, our purposes, our actions, will be in harmony with the will of God as expressed in the precepts of His holy law."—*Steps to Christ*, p. 61.

"Obedience is not a mere outward compliance but the service of love."—*Steps to Christ*, p. 60.

Walking with Jesus in loving obedience is not a matter of mere outward conformity to a set of rules and regulations. It involves much more than that. It involves our feelings, thoughts, purposes, and motives—those areas of our lives which are the spring of our actions and behavior.

"In the heart renewed by divine grace, love is the principle of action. It modifies the character, governs the impulses, controls the passions, subdues enmity, and ennobles the affections. This love, cherished in the soul, sweetens the life and sheds a refining influence on all around."—*Steps to Christ*, p. 59.

When God promises in terms of the new covenant to write His law in our hearts, what He is promising to do in effect is to break the control of the law of heredity over our lives (see Colossians 3:1-10, 15; and Romans 6:6-14) and to make the *principles of His divine law* the *principles of our characters,* so that henceforth our lives will be controlled, not by our passions and hereditary tendencies to sin, *but by principle*! These are the principles of His law:

1. Sincerity
2. Humility
3. Reverence
4. Loyalty
5. Respect
6. Pity and gentleness
7. Purity and fidelity
8. Honesty
9. Truthfulness
10. Contentment and unselfishness

These are the traits that will characterize the life of the new-covenant Christian. By His Spirit Christ makes them the very warp and woof of our characters. They become our life-style. *It's an exciting way to live!*

Chapter IV

The Ten Commandments are about God. Five times in the Ten Commandments God identifies Himself as "the Lord thy God." Exodus 20:2, 5, 7, 10, 12. If every other revelation of God were effaced from the earth and only the Ten Commandments remained, we would still know who God is. He would stand identified as the Only God (Exodus 20:3), the Unseen God (verse 11), the Just God (verse 5), the Merciful God (verse 6), the Creator (verse 11), the Deliverer (verse 2). We would know that He is the God above all gods (verse 3), above all matter (verses 4, 5), above all names (verse 7); that He is the God of time (verse 8-11), the God of the home (verse 12), the God of life (verse 13), the God of marriage (verse 14), the God of all things (verse 15), the God of truth (verse 16), the God who reads the innermost thoughts and intents of the heart (verse 17).

In the opening words of the law—"I AM"—He reveals Himself as the eternal God. His Uniqueness, His Spiritual Nature, His Justice, His Mercy, His Power to Create, His Power to Save, His Authority, His Sovereignty, His Greatness, His Nearness, His Eternity—all are revealed to us in His Ten Commandment law. This is why He spoke these unalterable precepts with His own voice (verse 1; cf. verse 19) and wrote them with His own hand (see Exodus 31:18; 32:16; Deuteronomy 5:22), instead of entrusting them to inspired messengers as with all other portions of Scripture. The eternal, unchanging, holy nature of this immutable law is stressed by the fact that it was uttered by the voice of Him and written by the hand of Him who is eternal, unchanging, and holy.

But above all, He is revealed in His law as The God of His people. He reveals Himself not merely as "The Lord God," but as 'The Lord thy God"—the God who wants to walk with us—and us to walk with Him!

The First Commandment

The first commandment is a call to worship Him alone, to give Him the exclusive, undivided devotion of our hearts. This call is echoed in the message of the first angel, recorded in Revelation 14:7, who proclaims: "Fear God, and give glory to him . . . : and worship him that made heaven, and earth, and the sea, and the fountains of waters."

In his book *God's Challenge to Modern Apostasy*, F. D. Nichol points out that the call is to worship *a personal God* who is *the Creator* of heaven and earth. No message could deal more directly with what he calls "the very heart of Bible religion, the bringing to men the truth regarding God as their Creator and the worship they should render to Him"—"a Creator who made this world for a purpose and to whom we owe our allegiance." In this connection he quotes a Congregational moderator who, speaking on modern man's great need to recover his sense of God, stated succinctly: "Men no longer believe in a sovereign God, a God who rules this world, and who by the hand of Moses issued a moral code for His subjects, and therefore that moral code has lost its binding authority. . . . The moral law is not something which we have invented. . . . I claim for it a higher authority than that. It derives from Almighty God. It comes to us as the expression of the will of the Creator and Ruler of this world."[1] Well said!

"The religion that comes from God is the only religion that will lead to God. In order to serve Him aright, we must be born of the divine Spirit. This will purify the heart and renew the mind, giving us a new capacity for knowing and loving God. It will give us a willing obedience to all His requirements. This is true worship. It is the fruit of the working of the Holy Spirit. By the Spirit every sincere prayer is indited, and such prayer is acceptable to God. Wherever a soul reaches out after God, there the Spirit's working is manifest, and God will reveal Himself to that soul. For such worshipers He is seeking. He waits to receive them, and to make them His sons and daughters."—*The Desire of Ages*, p. 189.

It is possible for even respectable, religious people to be idolaters and have "other gods" besides Him, without even realizing it! This is illustrated by the story of the encounter Jesus had with the rich young ruler: "And, behold, one came and said unto him, Good Master, what good thing shall I do, that I may have eternal life? And he said unto him, Why callest thou me good? there is none good but one, that is, God: but if thou wilt enter into life, keep the commandments. He saith unto him, Which? Jesus said, Thou shalt do no murder, Thou shalt not commit adultery, Thou shalt not steal, Thou shalt not bear false witness, Honour thy father and thy mother: and, Thou shalt love thy neighbor as thyself. The young man saith unto him, All these things have I kept from my youth up: what lack I yet? Jesus said unto him, If thou wilt be perfect, go and sell that thou hast, and give to the poor, and thou shalt have treasure in heaven: and come and follow me. But when the young man heard that saying, he went away sorrowful: for he had great possessions." Matthew 19:16-22.

"This man was tied to earth by the cords of his wealth. They did not hinder him from keeping the commandments, for he had no temptations to murder, or adultery, or theft, or neglect of parents. But they did hinder him from giving his whole self up, and from regarding eternal life as the most precious of all things. . . . The one thing needful for entrance into life is at bottom self-surrender, and the casting away of all else for its sovereign sake. . . . The hands must be emptied of treasures, and the heart swept clear of lesser loves, if He is to be grasped by our hands, and to dwell in our hearts. More of us than we are willing to believe are kept from entire surrender to Jesus Christ, by money and worldly possessions; and many professing Christians are kept shrivelled and weak and joyless because they love their wealth more than their Lord."[2]

In one of His parables Jesus described as a "fool" a person who makes a god of his possessions. See Luke 12:15-23.

Both the rich young ruler and the "rich fool" were probably respectable citizens who were held in high esteem in their community. There was nothing wrong with the fact that they were rich. What was wrong was that they placed "things" before God. They had their priorities wrong.

"Covetousness, or the greedy clutching at more and more of earthly goods, has its roots in us all, and unless there is the most assiduous weeding, it will overrun our whole nature. . . . We may be enslaved by it, and never suspect that we are. . . . Covetousness has many shapes, besides the grossest one of greed for money. . . . Not what we possess, but what we are, is the important matter."[3]

Writing under divine inspiration, the apostle Paul gives us a graphic description of mankind's idol-worshiping life-style in time's last hour. "This know also, that in the last days perilous times shall come. For men shall be lovers of their own selves, covetous, boasters, proud, blasphemers, disobedient to parents, unthankful, unholy, without natural affection, trucebreakers, false accusers, incontinent, fierce, despisers of those that are good, traitors, heady, highminded, lovers of pleasure more than lovers of God; having a form of godliness, but denying the power thereof: from such turn away." 2 Timothy 3:1-5.

The expression "men shall be lovers of their own selves . . . lovers of pleasure more than lovers of God" aptly portrays the pattern of life of a large proportion of earth's inhabitants in our day. The Bible does not condemn pleasure as such. God wants His people to enjoy genuine pleasure. We can be sure that all pleasure that is in harmony with His will, will only ever elevate and ennoble.

J. Wilbur Chapman gives us a simple rule to help us decide which are safe paths for our feet to walk on. "The rule that governs my life is this: Anything that dims my vision of Christ, or takes away my taste for Bible study, or cramps my prayer life, or makes Christian work difficult, is wrong for me, and I must, as a Christian, turn away from it."

The picture that Paul portrays in the passage of Scripture quoted above is of people who are living to satisfy the senses rather than to please God. Whenever this happens, "pleasure" becomes another of modern man's false gods, which, like all false gods, becomes degrading and depraving. See Romans 1:21-32.

The Question of Images

The second commandment forbids the making of graven images as objects of worship. It is interesting to observe that, with the exception of the fourth, more words are used by God in expounding this second precept of the law than on any of the others: "Thou shalt not make unto thee any graven image, or any likeness of any thing that is in the heaven above, or that is in the earth beneath, or that is in the water under the earth: thou shalt not bow down thyself to them, nor serve them: for I the Lord thy God am a jealous God, visiting the iniquity of the fathers upon the children unto the third and fourth generation of them that hate me; and showing mercy unto thousands of them that love me, and keep my commandments." Exodus 20:4-6.

The people whom God had called out of Egyptian bondage to be His special people were surrounded on every hand by heathen nations who bestowed their worship on created objects instead of on the Creator. The reason for this was that sin had so warped their spiritual perceptions that their carnal, unsanctified, proud hearts could not grasp the unseen God. They substituted the seen for the unseen. Is this pagan tendency very far removed from the rationalism of our day which is prepared to accept only what can be demonstrated to the natural senses?

The truth underlying the second commandment is that at the heart of all true religion is a *sixth sense* that reaches out like an invisible hand to search out and find the unseen God who is beyond the range of mortal sight, sound, speech, smell, and touch. This sixth sense the Bible calls faith.

What is faith? The most concise definition is found in Hebrews 11:1—"And what is faith? Faith gives substance to our hopes and makes us certain of realities we do not see." (My translation.) It then goes on to stress the importance of faith in maintaining true religion: "Without faith it is impossible to please him: for anyone who comes to God must believe that he exists and that he rewards those who search for him." Verse 6, NEB.

Belief in God is logical, but He cannot be proved by logic. Logic is like the first elevator in the Eiffel Tower in Paris which takes you just so far. Then, if you would go to the top, you must take the second elevator. In Christian experience this second elevator is faith. This is the elevator that takes you to the top!

Among the pagans of Israel's day—and our own—this second elevator had broken down. It had been demolished by human philosophy and by the sophistries of pride and sin. Sin always keeps men from getting through to God. And when the hardness of their own hearts veils God from their spiritual sight, they begin to invent substitutes and crutches which will satisfy the carnal heart. Satan has absolutely no objection to men worshiping, as long as they do not worship the true God. On the contrary, he will encourage men to worship any object their imagination can possibly devise, so long as the toys of their imagination can keep them from the One who is to be the sole object of worship, the unseen Creator of the seen creation. The central issue at stake in the second commandment is Creator-worship versus creature-worship—the worship of the Unseen versus the worship of the seen.

The Egyptians, among whom the Israelites had lived as slaves for so many generations, shared with their contemporaries in the universal worship of the visible creation. One of the objects of their worship was the River Nile, which brought fertility and life to their country. Hence it was to them the symbol of fertility and life. Everything that came out of the Nile was sacred. So, they worshiped the frog. An Egyptian was not permitted to kill a frog; it was a gift of their river god. This is why the first two plagues touched their Nilotic object of worship. In the first plague the waters of the river were turned to blood and rendered undrinkable. In the second, the land was infested with frogs. Thus the Egyptians were to learn that the Creator was superior to the creature. "That thou mayest know how that the earth is the Lord's." Exodus 9:29.

Among the other nations there were similar objects of worship. A study of the gods of the nations through the ages could fill a book. In a sentence: They were all variations of the same departure—creature-worship in place of Creator-worship, the worship of the visible instead of the Invisible. It is worthy of note that each object of worship was in turn a symbol of fertility and hence of life. This held true whether the object worshiped was the river, the sun, or a woman. It was against this substitution of a creature-symbol for the true Source of life who is above all human symbolism that God emphatically warned His people.

The worship of creature-representations reached its peak during the golden age of Greco-Roman civilization. The Roman pantheon contained gods representing every sphere of human experience—a god of war, a god of peace, a goddess of fertility and love, to mention only a few.

What happened next is almost inevitable. As Christianity, which had been built on the foundations of the Judaistic concept of the worship of the unseen Creator, encountered Greco-Roman creature-worship, it gradually began to absorb into its system the elements of Rome's false religion. Gradually the Christian church drifted from the simplicity of the gospel. As it lost its vital faith in the Unseen it began to rely more and more on the seen.

The apostle Paul met this object-worshiping idolatry head-on in the course of his missionary travels. In Athens he sought to draw the minds of his listeners on Mars Hill from visible concepts of deity to the concept of an unseen God. See Acts 17:23-28.

"The city of Athens was the metropolis of heathendom. Here Paul did not meet with an ignorant, credulous populace, as at Lystra, but with a people famous for their intelligence and culture. Everywhere statues of their gods and of the deified heroes of history and poetry met the eye, while magnificent architecture and paintings represented the national glory and the popular worship of heathen deities. . . .

"As Paul looked upon the beauty and grandeur surrounding him, and saw the city wholly given to idolatry, his spirit was stirred with jealousy for God, whom he saw dishonored on every side, and his heart was drawn out in pity for the people of Athens, who, not withstanding their intellectual culture, were ignorant of the true God. . . .

"Paul drew the minds of his idolatrous hearers beyond the limits of their false religion to a true view of the Deity, whom they had styled the 'Unknown God.' This Being, whom he now declared unto them, was independent of man, needing nothing from human hands to add to His power and glory."—*The Acts of the Apostles*, pp. 233-238.

The testimony of Scripture and of history is that the worship of material objects as representations of deity always degrades the devotee of the object to a level even lower than the object worshiped. Those systems of religion that sponsor creature-worship instead of Creator-worship always lead their devotees to gross animalism and perversion. That is why sex-worship, accompanied by sexual orgies and licentiousness, has always been a companion of sun-worship, creature-worship, and idol-worship.

Man never rises any higher than the god he serves. When the object of his worship is an animal, that will be the level of his life. When a man turns to serve the living God—the Unseen, the Eternal—his soul expands to the dimensions of his quest. He becomes a partaker "of the divine nature." 2 Peter 1:4.

How often we have seen this happen in the lives of primitive, cannibalistic, demon-worshipers! They are the umpteenth generation of people who know not God. The natural law of heredity is at work in them—destroying, depraving, degrading. Then the gospel finds them. They turn from the creature to the Creator. By faith they learn to love and serve the unseen, eternal God. He shows them mercy. Even Charles Darwin was so amazed at the transformation wrought in the lives of the Patagonians, whom he described as the most primitive and depraved peoples he had seen anywhere in his travels, that to the end of his life he continued to be a contributor to the Foreign Missions Board!

"In the first chapter of Romans, Paul gives a vivid account of the moral downfall of the race. The key to the mystery of how men made in the image of God could ever descend to the immoral depths of paganism, is found in the fact that 'they refused to have God in their knowledge.' Verse 28. The whole narrative in the preceeding verses emphasizes this thought in variant forms. The decline began 'because that, when they knew God, they glorified Him not as God.' Verse 21. They forgot Him as the Creator. They 'exchanged the truth of God for a lie, and worshiped and served the creature rather than the Creator.' Verse 25."[4]

This, of course, is Satan's whole purpose—the animalization of the human race and the entire defacement of the image of God in man! Fortunately the converse is also true! The worship of the true God expands the intellect, elevates the soul, and ennobles the character of the worshiper!

Substitutes for Faith

Visible and tangible man-made representations of deity tend to become spiritual crutches and hence substitutes for faith. By daring to represent the infinite, invisible, incomprehensible, and eternal God by finite, visible, and interpretable forms and symbols, man in his arrogance drags the Creator down to the level of the creature. Not only is such an exercise destructive of faith and conducive to human pride, but it is stifling to character develoment and hence morally degrading.

God desires our walk with Him to be without crutches! He has given us revelations of Himself to strengthen our faith. But these are not representations of Himself on which to lean. He reveals Himself to us in His Word, the Bible. He reveals Himself through Jesus Christ, the God-man; through the movings of the Holy Spirit, in answers to prayer and the fulfillments of His promises. By availing ourselves of these provisions, we can cultivate a precious personal fellowship with the God whom our eyes have never seen.

Captain Howard Rutledge discovered the importance of utilizing these faith-developing avenues of communion with God during his seven years as a prisoner of war in North Vietnam. He says: "I had completely neglected the spiritual dimension of my life. It took prison to show me how empty life is without God. . . . I tried desperately to recall snatches of Scripture, sermons, the gospel choruses from childhood, and the hymns we sang in church. . . . How I struggled to recall those Scriptures and hymns! Regrettably I had not seen the importance of memorizing verses from the Bible or learning gospel songs. I never dreamed that I would spend almost seven years (five of them in solitary confinement) in a prison in North Vietnam or that thinking about one memorized verse could have made a whole day bearable. One portion of a verse I did remember was, 'Thy word have I hid in my heart.' How often I wished I had really worked to hide God's Word in my heart. . . . I cannot explain with reason or proof why my faith was central to my survival. But it was. . . . For me faith in Christ made all the difference."[5]

How desperately every one of us needs to make the same vital discovery! "Through faith, which is the highest exercise of the human mind guided by divine revelation, we understand the mysteries of God the Creator. Faith never stands against reason; it always illuminates it. Through faith we understand. Reason becomes graphic as a result of faith in God. . . . God as Creator gives purpose to every breath we take and to every thought we think."[6]

"God never asks us to park our minds outside when we enter the church to worship Him."[7]

"If a man says, 'I must have full proof or I refuse to believe in God,' what is proof? The proof of God comes out of a man's experience as he listens to the divine Voice speaking through the created works of nature, through the Bible, and through the life and death of Jesus Christ. Faith grows from inside the life. When it is rich and strong, man exclaims as did Job, 'I know that my Redeemer liveth!' "[8]

Works of Art

The second commandment does not condemn works of art; it only forbids the fashioning of representations of divinity for veneration or worship. This is borne out by the fact that when God gave Moses details for the construction of the earthly tabernacle, He included representations of angels and many objects from the natural world among the items which made up the furnishings and decoration of the tabernacle. See Exodus 25 to 40 and Leviticus 4 and 16. The factor that makes the fashioning of any representation of God wrong is that it limits the God who is totally unlimited and illimitable.

No material representation of God, or combination of representations, could possibly portray or depict the God who is unlimited in power, in space, in time, in love, in majesty, or in sovereignty. Any effort to whittle the eternal God down to the dimensions of our puny understanding is sin. It is this limitation that is condemned by the second commandment and by the total testimony of Scripture. What God wants us to concentrate our attention on is to grasp and appreciate as fully as possible the beauty and steadfastness of His character. He wants us to love Him not for what He looks like, but for who He is!

A Warning and a Promise

The second commandment reveals two of the main attributes of God's character—His justice and His mercy. "Thou shalt not bow down thyself to them, nor serve them: for I the Lord thy God am a jealous God, visiting the iniquity of the fathers upon the children unto the third and fourth generation of them that hate me; and shewing mercy unto thousands of them that love me, and keep my commandments." Exodus 20:5, 6.

"It is inevitable that children should suffer from the consequences of parental wrongdoing, but they are not punished for the parent's guilt, except as they participate in their sins. It is usually the case, however, that children walk in the steps of their parents. By inheritance and example the sons become partakers of the father's sin. Wrong tendencies, perverted appetites, and debased morals, as well as physical disease and degeneracy, are transmitted as a legacy from father to son, to the third and fourth generation. This fearful truth should have a solemn power to restrain men from following a course of sin.

"And to those who are faithful in His service, mercy is promised, not merely to the third and fourth generation as is the wrath threatened against those who hate Him, but to *thousands* of generations."—*Patriarchs and Prophets*, p. 306.

The second commandment ends with a promise! "Shewing mercy unto thousands of them that love me, and keep my commandments." No matter how godless your heritage may be, the Almighty stands ready to reverse a natural law of heredity on behalf of those who turn to serve Him with all their hearts! The law of heredity that operates in you to destruction will be replaced in your being by a new law—"the law of the Spirit of life in Christ Jesus." Romans 8:2. As your soul reaches out for the eternal God, the Creator, He will reach down into your life and transform your character into His likeness.

It is a law of life that the gods we serve mold us into their likeness. You will observe that those who worship money, pleasure, appetite, fashion, self, or whatever, bear the stamp of their god on their characters. This fact contains a promise to all who with sincere hearts worship the God of heaven. "His servants shall serve him: and they shall see his face; and his name shall be in their foreheads." Revelation 22:3, 4. "Him that overcometh will I make a pillar in the temple of my God, . . . and I will write upon him the name of my God." Revelation 3:12. That's what He wants to do for you and me. Shall we let Him?

Chapter V

No commandment of the ten is more lightly, thoughtlessly, or heedlessly transgressed than the one which safeguards the holiness of God's name. A man may refrain from stealing because he fears being caught. He may shrink from murder because he fears the law. He may hesitate to commit adultery because he is afraid of endangering his marriage or of other social consequences. But when it comes to that prohibition which says, "Thou shalt not take the name of the Lord thy God in vain" (Exodus 20:7), there is no statutory law by which a court on earth can condemn him.

Yet the transgression of no other commandment is more inexcusable. A man may steal because he is hungry. He may commit murder because he is driven by extenuating circumstances. He may be trapped into adultery through loneliness or other emotional factors. Saying this does not imply that these things justify his sinful course of action. They attempt to explain but do not excuse the wrong. When it comes to profanity, however, no reasonable excuse can be offered for its commission.

Why then do men presume to drag the most exalted name to the lowest level? Why should this holiest name be used as an epithet in every bar, gambling den, nightclub, brothel, alley, gutter, and slum? Why is it the handy adjective in every sphere of human relationship—sports, commerce, industry, education, social activity, or intellectual pursuit? Why should this holiest name be a part of the jargon of every circle of society—of the sailor, the dockyard worker, the plumber, the professional man, and the scholar?

We can find only one answer to this question: This commandment, above all others, reveals the true condition of a man's heart. The commandment "Thou shalt not steal" may not fully reveal this. A man may refrain from stealing, not because he is innately honest, but because "honesty is the best policy." He may be kept from adultery, not because his heart is intrinsically pure, but because decency is the expected thing in the sphere in which he revolves, or he may fear the social consequences. But when a man's heart is right, it will be revealed in his speech. And if his heart is *not* right, no amount of religious camouflage will be able to keep the fact from showing through his speech in times of stress. A man's words, then, reveal, as nothing else can, the *quality* of his life and his religion.

The Bible abounds with statements that underscore this truth. Jesus declared:

"Out of the abundance of the heart the mouth speaketh. A good man out of the good treasure of the heart bringeth forth good things: and an evil man out of the evil treasure bringeth forth evil things." "For by thy words thou shalt be justified, and by thy words thou shalt be condemned." Matthew 12:34, 35, 37. James, the brother of Jesus, makes this profound statement: "If any man offend not in word, the same is a perfect man." James 3:2.

Profanity, then, is not the disease, but merely the symptom thereof. The rash is not the measles; it is the outward evidence that there is something wrong inside.

A man who uses God's name in vain does so because he has no conception of God's holiness. It's no use telling him he shouldn't. Telling him he shouldn't is like trying to cure measles by treating the rash. What is needed is for the life to be changed from within. Man needs a vision of God.

Notice what such a vision did for Isaiah. In chapter 6 of the prophecy that bears his name, he tells us of a vision he had of the holiness of God: "In the year that king Uzziah died I saw also the Lord sitting upon a throne, high and lifted up, and his train filled the temple. Above it stood the seraphims: each one had six wings; with twain he covered his face, and with twain he covered his feet, and with twain he did fly. And one cried unto another, and said, Holy, holy, holy, is the Lord of hosts: the whole earth is full of his glory. And the posts of the door moved at the voice of him that cried, and the house was filled with smoke." Isaiah 6:1-4. In the next verse he hastens on to tell us his reaction to this awesome revelation of God's majesty: "Then said I, Woe is me! for I am undone; because I am a man of unclean lips, and I dwell in the midst of a people of unclean lips: for mine eyes have seen the King, the Lord of hosts." Isaiah 6:5.

It is noteworthy, however, that God's revelation of His holiness was not intended to devastate Isaiah. God reveals Himself to us to humble us, never to humiliate us. There is a difference. When a man is humbled he senses his need but seeks to have that need supplied; he feels helpless but not hopeless. When a man is humiliated he feels devastated and beyond hope. The revelation of God's holiness never devastates. It brings healing.

This is beautifully brought out in what immediately follows Isaiah's glimpse of God's holiness. "Then flew one of the seraphims unto me, having a live coal in his hand, which he had taken with the tongs from off the altar: and he laid it upon my mouth, and said, Lo, this hath touched thy lips; and thine iniquity is taken away, and thy sin purged. Also I heard the voice of the Lord, saying, Whom shall I send, and who will go for us? Then said I, Here am I; send me." Isaiah 6:6-8.

It is significant that the vision of God's holiness did not disqualify but qualified Isaiah for usefulness. This is always God's purpose in revealing Himself to men.

Moses was likewise prepared for his God-appointed mission by being given a realization of the Lord's holiness.

Moses "was warned not to approach irreverently: 'Put off thy shoes from off thy feet; for the place whereon thou standest is holy ground.' . . .

"Humility and reverence should characterize the deportment of all who come into the presence of God. In the name of Jesus we may come before Him with confidence, but we must not approach Him with the boldness of presumption, as though He were on a level with ourselves. There are those who address the great and all-powerful and holy God, who dwelleth in light unapproachable, as they would address an equal, or even an inferior. There are those who conduct themselves in His house as they would not presume to do in the audience chamber of an earthly ruler. These should remember that they are in His sight whom seraphim adore, before whom angels veil their faces. God is greatly to be reverenced; all who truly realize His presence will bow in humility before Him, and, like Jacob beholding the vision of God, they will cry out, 'How dreadful is this place! This is none other but the house of God, and this is the gate of heaven.' "—*Patriarchs and Prophets*, pp. 251, 252.

Hallowed Be Thy Name

Jesus taught us the holiness of God's name by incorporating the truth into the Lord's Prayer. "After this manner therefore pray ye: Our Father which art in heaven, Hallowed be thy name." Matthews 6:9.

Says one Christian writer: "To hallow the name of the Lord requires that the words in which we speak of the Supreme Being be uttered with reverence. . . . We are never in any manner to treat lightly the titles or appellations of the Deity. In prayer we enter the audience chamber of the Most High; and we should come before Him with holy awe. The angels veil their faces in His presence. The cherubim and the bright and holy seraphim approach His throne with solemn reverence. How much more should we, finite, sinful beings, come in a reverent manner before the Lord, our Maker."—*Thoughts From the Mount of Blessing*, p. 106.

It is possible to profane the name of God by even using it too frequently in prayer! Notice the counsel Jesus gave us on "vain repetitions." "But when ye pray, use not vain repetitions, as the heathen do: for they think that they shall be heard for their much speaking. Be not ye therefore like unto them: for your Father knoweth what things ye have need of, before ye ask him." Matthew 6:7, 8.

It is interesting to observe that in the sixth chapter of Matthew—the chapter in which is recorded the prayer aspect of Christ's Sermon on the Mount—the name of God occurs only three times (verses 24, 30, and 33), while terms such as your Father, thy Father, our Father, your heavenly Father, occur twelve times (verses 1, 4, 6, 8, 9, 14, 15, 18, 26, 32). The conclusion is obvious that the favored title for God by which Jesus taught us to address Him is Father. This does two things for us. It reminds us that the God to whom we come in prayer is loving, merciful, and gracious, a type of what earthly fathers should be toward their children. Second, when we use this term we acknowledge that we are His children. We cannot call Him Father without acknowledging our sonship and daughtership. This relationship in turn will create in us the desire and determination to be worthy of that high honor.

Forms of Profanity

The profaning of God's name has many variations and refinements in our day and age. A person may unwittingly use expressions that have been taught him without realizing that he is sinning. Examine the expressions *you* use as epithets and pray for divine enlightenment as to whether perhaps you are unwittingly using the name of God in vain, in disguised forms. If you find that you are, seek God's forgiveness and then ask Him to help you overcome the habit to which you have become enslaved. The surest way there is of avoiding the snare of unsuspectingly transgressing the third commandment is to avoid all slang expressions. By so doing you will steer clear of those borderline expressions that verge on profanity.

The care we need to exercise in avoiding the misuse of the holiest of all names becomes clear as we ponder the rendering of the third commandment of the decalogue in a number of contemporary translations:

"Do not use my name for evil purposes, because I, the LORD your God, will punish anyone who misuses my name." TEV.

"You shall not make wrong use of the name of the Lord your God; the LORD will not leave unpunished the man who misuses his name." NEB

"You shall not use the name of the Eternal, your God, profanely; for the Eternal will never acquit anyone who uses his name profanely." Moffatt.

"You shall not misuse the name of the Lord your God, for the Lord will not hold anyone guiltless who misuses his name." NIV.

"You are not to make use of the name of the Lord your God for an evil purpose; whoever takes the Lord's name on his lips for an evil purpose will be judged a sinner by the Lord." Basic English Version.

Reverencing God's Name in My Life

"When you pray, 'Hallowed be Thy name,' you ask that it may be hallowed in this world, hallowed in you. God has acknowledged you before men and angels as His child; pray that you may do no dishonor to the 'worthy name by which ye are called.' James 2:7. God sends you into the world as His representative. In every act of life you are to make manifest the name of God. This petition calls upon you to possess His character. You cannot hallow His name, you cannot represent Him to the world, unless in life and character you represent the very life and character of God. This you can do only through the acceptance of the grace and righteousness of Christ."—*Thoughts From the Mount of Blessing*, p. 107.

The Final Call

In time's last hour the message that rings out to the inhabitants of earth is a call to reverence God. To fear God, in the biblical sense, does not mean to be afraid of Him, but to hold Him in awe. Three verbs are used in succession in Revelation 14:7—*fear, give glory*, and *worship*. A fourth is added in Ecclesiastes 12:13—"*keep* his commandments." The injunction to "*fear*" God is thus a call to worship. True worship will result in our glorifying Him in our lives and in our obeying Him. The sequence of the verbs reveals that to "fear" God is not a negative experience, else it would not result in the powerful positives of giving glory and rendering worship. God never frightens us into serving Him. Rather He gives us in His Word a sense of His holiness. This will result in our reverencing and obeying Him. Obedience to God should be the result of our grasping with our minds His supreme holiness. The basis of His appeal to us to be holy, is His own holiness. "And ye shall be holy unto me: for I the Lord am holy, and have severed you from other people, that ye should be mine." Leviticus 20:26.

"Christ's followers today should guard against the tendency to lose the spirit of reverence and godly fear. The Scriptures teach men how they should approach their Maker—with humility and awe, through faith in a divine Mediator.

"True reverence for God is inspired by a sense of His infinite greatness and a realization of His presence. With this sense of the Unseen, every heart should be deeply impressed. The hour and place of prayer are sacred, because God is there. And as reverence is manifested in attitude and demeanor, the feeling that inspires it will be deepened. 'Holy and reverend is His name,' the psalmist declares. Psalm 111:9. Angels, when they speak that name, veil their faces. With what reverence, then, should we, who are fallen and sinful, take it upon our lips!"—*Prophets and Kings*, pp. 48, 49.

Professing to be Christians, while our lives are a standing denial of our profession, is more than hypocrisy and deception. It is in fact blasphemy—a violation of the third commandment—for those who practice this are in a very real sense taking the Lord's name in vain. Little wonder then that victory over profanity and blasphemy is an essential qualification for entrance into the kingdom of God. Concerning the redeemed, the prophet John was given this description in Revelation 14:5: "And in their mouth was found no guile [no hypocrisy, no deceptiveness]: for they are without fault before the throne of God."

This may seem like a discouragingly high ideal! But remember that God's biddings are enablings. When God sets this ideal before us, He provides with the challenge the grace and the divine resources to attain it. Yes, He really means that at the end of time, in an age of abandoned, reckless blasphemy, He is going to have a people who are blameless in their speech—they live up to their profession of being Christians. And the prize is certainly worth the effort. Through all eternity these guileless ones will stand with the Lamb on the Mount Zion. Revelation 14:1.

But while we wait for that day, we have the incomparable privilege of "giving glory" to God here and now—in our speech, in our lives, in our deportment. I can't think of any higher joy that could possibly come to a human being in time's last hour than to have a part in that assignment!

Chapter VI

There are very few things God commands us to remember. The word *remember* is used as an imperative in the Bible no more than half a dozen times. We are commanded to remember all His "marvellous works." See 1 Chronicles 16:12; Psalm 105:5. We are commanded to "remember the days of old," to "consider the years of many generations." Deuteronomy 32:7. The youth are commanded to "remember now thy Creator in the days of thy youth." Ecclesiastes 12:1. Jesus commands us to "remember Lot's wife." Luke 17:32.

The imperative, *remember,* suggests two things: First, that forgetting is so easy! Second, that the thing we are commanded to remember is of momentous importance. When God says, "Remember," He wants us to know that in His estimation, it is of great concern that we should remember!

One of the important things God commands us to remember is the Sabbath. The fact underlying its importance is that it is a memorial to God's creatorship—a memorial to the fact that God is the Creator of heaven and earth.

"Remember the sabbath day, to keep it holy. . . . The seventh day is the sabbath of the Lord thy God: . . . for in six days the Lord made heaven and earth, the sea, and all that in them is, and rested the seventh day: wherefore the Lord blessed the sabbath day, and hallowed it." Exodus 20:8-11.

It is this fundamental fact that God is the Creator, that gives Him His right to rule. Notice what the Bible declares: "Thou are worthy, O Lord, to receive glory and honour and power: for thou hast created all things, and for thy pleasure they are and were created." Revelation 4:11. Compare Jeremiah 10:7, 10-12; 27:5.

Arthur Bietz uses a vivid word picture to portray the deep significance of God's creatorship: "The origin of life on the earth and the marvelous way it is developed and maintained, demands a Creator.

"The manifestations of the human intellect must presuppose a supreme Intelligence behind the human. As one scientist declares: 'Of all the incomprehensible things in the universe, man stands in the front rank, and of all the incomprehensible things in man, the supreme difficulty centers in the human brain, intelligence, memory, aspiration, power of discovery, research, and conquest of obstacles. Man has ten thousand million brain cells, and all of these can form an infinite number of connections and combinations. Was it merely chance that wrought the human brain?'

"So many conditions are necessary for life, that it is impossible that chance could have put all of them in their proper relationship on earth at one time.

"The complex structure of the atom, with its more than thirty different types of infinitesimal components,—protons, electrons, neutrons, and the like,—the highly complex nature of protein molecules, and the wonder of the cells of the human body, all point to a special creation.

"Suppose you take ten pennies, mark them from 1 to 10, and place them in your pocket. Now give them a good shake, and try to draw them out in exact sequence from 1 to 10. . . . Your chance of drawing numbers 1 and 2 in succession is 1 in 100. Your chance of drawing numbers 1, 2, 3 in succession is 1 in 1000. But to draw out 1 to 10 in succession is almost an impossibility. From this simple act, turn to the complex organization of the universe. How plainly impossible that our universe, with its laws of nature and life, should all have come about by chance!

"Our atmosphere is composed of nitrogen, oxygen, argon, carbon dioxide, hydrogen, neon, helium, krypton, and xenon. Seventy-eight percent is nitrogen; 21 percent is oxygen. This is the proportion necessary to life. If there were 50 percent oxygen instead of 21 percent, all things would become inflammable, so that if lightning were to strike a tree, the whole forest would explode.

If there were much less than 21 percent, we could not build a fire.

"There is not one chance in millions that all the conditions necessary to our life on earth should have just happened. Science has no explanation for these facts.

"The Bible gives the straightforward answer in these words: 'He hath made the earth by His power, He hath established the world by His wisdom, and hath stretched out the heaven by His understanding.' Jeremiah 51:15."[9]

If we just "came about by chance," to whom are we accountable? If, on the other hand, we were created by a supremely wise and powerful Being to whom we owe the very privilege of existence, do we not also owe Him our allegiance?

"The Sabbath, as a memorial of God's creative power, points to Him as the maker of the heavens and the earth. Hence it is a constant witness to His existence and a reminder of His greatness, His wisdom, and His love. Had the Sabbath always been sacredly observed, there could never have been an atheist or an idolater.

"The Sabbath institution, which originated in Eden, is as old as the world itself. It was observed by all the patriarchs, from creation down. During the bondage in Egypt, the Israelites were forced by their taskmasters to violate the Sabbath, and to a great extent they lost the knowledge of its sacredness. When the law was proclaimed at Sinai the very first words of the fourth commandment were, 'Remember the Sabbath day, to keep it holy'—showing that the Sabbath was not then instituted; we are pointed back for its origin to creation. In order to obliterate God from the minds of men, Satan aimed to tear down this great memorial. If men could be led to forget their Creator, they would make no effort to resist the power of evil, and Satan would be sure of his prey."—*Patriarchs and Prophets*, p. 336.

Instituted in Eden

The institution of the Sabbath goes right back to the Garden of Eden. Concerning the establishment of this divine institution, the Bible says, "Thus the heavens and the earth were finished, and all the host of them. And on the seventh day God ended his work which he had made. . . . And God blessed the seventh day, and sanctified it: because that in it he had rested from all his work which God created and made." Genesis 2:1-3.

We have heard it argued that there is nothing in this passage which states that God gave the seventh day to mankind as a sabbath at this stage. It was merely God who is said to have rested. There is no record that man rested or that he was commanded by God to do so. We have need therefore to refer the reader to the wording so specifically used: "And God blessed the seventh day, *and sanctified it*." Genesis 2:3. Emphasis supplied. To sanctify means to set apart for a sacred purpose. It is clearly with reference to "every thing that he had made" (Genesis 1:31) that God sanctified the Sabbath. The evidence of Scripture on this point is very clear: It was not with reference to Himself that He created the Sabbath, but with reference to the man whom He had created in His image. Verse 27. Jesus made this clear when He said, "The sabbath was made for man." Mark 2:27. The purpose of the Sabbath is further clarified in Ezekiel 20:12 and 20: "Moreover also I gave them my sabbaths, to be a sign between me and them, that they might know that I am the Lord that sanctify them." "And hallow my sabbaths; and they shall be a sign between me and you, that ye may know that I am the Lord your God." Notice that the Sabbath was to be a sign between God and His people. This was obviously its intention from the very beginning of time.

But, asks some reader, why is there no specific record of Sabbath keeping on earth or of a Sabbath command until the time of the Exodus? Does this not indicate that mankind did not keep a Sabbath until the Israelites did so in the wilderness? In answer to this question one must bear in mind that until Moses *there was no written record at all*! The decrees and revelations of the Almighty were handed down through succeeding generations from father to son. One has but to remember that every one of Adam's posterity until Noah was born during Adam's lifetime, to realize how perfectly the knowledge of God's will was relayed through succeeding generations. One needs also to remember that the first 2300 years of human history is covered in forty brief chapters of Holy Writ. It stands to reason that only the broadest outline, not the minutest details, were placed on record. What was obvious did not need to be restated. That God had "sanctified" a Sabbath for the use of His people was one of those obvious facts. When we bear these things in mind, we are seeing the early history of God's dealings with the race in perspective; and the problem concerning what is not directly stated, but is clearly implied, falls away.

It was only after God's people had been subjected to generations of slavery in a foreign land and had had their spiritual perceptions warped and obscured during their "dark ages" of bondage that they needed to be reminded of what their forefathers had believed, taught, and practiced. The Exodus was to be not only Israel's deliverance but also their renaissance. All the sacred treasures that had been handed down to them by their fathers and then lost in slavery were now to be restored—including Jehovah's Sabbath, the memorial of Creation.

The Wording and Position of the Fourth Commandment

Notice the precise wording of this commandment: "Remember the sabbath day, to keep it holy. Six days shalt thou labour, and do all thy work: but the seventh day is the sabbath of the Lord thy God: in it thou shalt not do any work, thou, nor thy son, nor thy daughter, thy manservant, nor thy maidservant, nor thy cattle, nor thy stranger that is within thy gates: for in six days the Lord made heaven and earth, the sea, and all that in them is, and rested the seventh day: wherefore the Lord blessed the sabbath day, and hallowed it." Exodus 20:8-11.

Let us consider some significant aspects of this commandment:

1. It is the only commandment of the ten that begins with the word *remember*. There are good reasons why God chose to use the word *remember* in connection with the Sabbath commandment. The first is that it is so easy to forget. (And how completely the world *has* forgotten!) Second it points to the fact that God was reiterating something that they already knew about. If I say to my son, "Remember to put seed and water in the birdcage today," I imply that I have already instructed him concerning this requirement. I would not tell him to "remember" to do something he did not already know about! Yes, Israel knew all about the Sabbath all right. Their fathers had kept it. Now they were to keep it. They were not to forget it. They were to "remember."

2. God saw fit to place the Sabbath commandment in the heart

of His law, where nothing would ever be able to dislodge it from its place. If it had been placed first or last, some person anxious to remove this embarrassing commandment from God's law might have argued that it didn't really belong but that it had been appended by some scribe by mistake! So God put it in the middle, where no man can ever chop it out without chopping a hole clear through the center of the sacred table!

3. God also saw fit to expend as many words on this commandment as on eight of the others put together! Not only does He tell us how to keep it, but also why to keep it. The reason is Creation: "For in six days the Lord made heaven and earth, the sea, and all that in them is, and rested the seventh day: wherefore the Lord blessed the sabbath day, and hallowed it." Exodus 20:11. Every time His people kept the Sabbath of the Creator, they would be reminded of the Creator of the Sabbath! This is made clear in Exodus 31:17. "It is a sign between me and the children of Israel for ever: for in six days the Lord made heaven and earth, and on the seventh day he rested, and was refreshed."

Does this mean that only the nation of Israel was to keep the Sabbath? Bear in mind that in pre-Messianic times the nation of Israel was the church. See Acts 7:38. When God said that Israel was to keep His Sabbath, He was virtually saying, in language we would use today, "The members of the church shall keep the Sabbath." It was to be kept by His church in pre-Messianic days, and it is to be kept by His church today.

4. The commandment does not call for the keeping of *a* Sabbath, but for the keeping of "*the* Sabbath." It is the observance of a specified day that is called for. That day is the day God blessed, hallowed, and sanctified. A man may say, "Well, as long as I keep one day in seven, it matters not whether I keep Monday, Wednesday, or Friday." Does it matter? Let us illustrate it this way: A man may say, "If I hang a piece of rag in front of my house I am still flying the flag. It matters not whether the rag is yellow, green, blue, or red. As long as it's a bit of rag, it's still a flag!" Is that man flying the flag or not? Is he a patriotic citizen? You see, it's not the rag that has any significance. It's what the rag stands for that makes of the rag a flag! Only one authority has the power to create a flag—the government of a country! Supposing each citizen of

the land had a different flag, and each one said his flag was the right one, how would we know which was the authentic one? Simple! Go to the statute book and see which is the flag that has been ordained by the government. Dear reader, there is only one power who has the authority to create a Sabbath. That One is the Creator of heaven and earth—the God of the universe. We may be ever so pious and sincere in our observance of a particular day, but unless we observe the day God ordained at Creation and in His law, we are not keeping the Sabbath!

What a Flag Symbolizes

The story is told of a Frenchman who changed his nationality and became an Englishman. The day after his nationalization, his friends asked him what difference his new nationality made to him. After reflection he replied, "Yesterday Waterloo was a defeat. Today Waterloo is a victory!"

He might also have said, "Yesterday the Tricolor was my flag and the Union Jack was a foreign flag, whereas today the Tricolor is a foreign flag and the Union Jack is *my* flag."

A flag has tremendous significance, for while it is merely a "piece of rag" it symbolizes all that a country stands for. It represents a country's government, its authority, its culture, its history, its sovereignty, its laws, its people, its ideals, its principles, its life-style, its character, in fact, everything that constitutes it as a nation.

The flag I fly designates my loyalty and my allegiance to a particular country. If I were to unfurl the flag of another country over the soil of my country, I would clearly be indicating that I had no love for or allegiance to my country and that my loyalty was to the country whose flag I was flying. If such a flag belonged to a country against which my country happened to be at war, I would be announcing in clearest terms that my sympathies were on the side of my country's enemies, and I would be called a traitor. The flying of the enemy's flag would not be regarded lightly. It would be accepted as a sign of my enmity toward my own country and its government. The flag I fly is, then, the sign of whose side I'm on!

The Bible says that the Sabbath is such a sign between God and His people. Let us read again Ezekiel 20:12, 20: "Moreover also I gave them my sabbaths, to be a sign between me and them, that they might know that I am the Lord that sanctify them." "And hallow my sabbaths; and they shall be a sign between me and you, that ye may know that I am the Lord your God."

These are powerful words. They cannot be lightly set aside. God is virtually saying that what a flag stands for in relationship between a man and his country, the Sabbath stands for in the covenant relationship between Himself and His people. "What's in a day? Surely one day is as good as another," someone says. Dear friend, it isn't merely a matter of "a day." It's what that day stands for! The thing that sets the Sabbath apart as something uniquely sacred, sacredly unique, is that God the Creator set it up as a sign between Himself and His people. He says so.

Now supposing some other party, any other party, were to come along and institute another day in the place of the one God ordained—unfurl another flag over His people, as it were—what would the implications of such an act be? You know the answer.

Centuries ago the prophet Daniel predicted that just such a thing would happen! Read it in Daniel 7:25: "And he shall speak great words against the most High, and shall wear out the saints of the most High, and think to change times and laws." Some other translations say, "the times in the law." The only commandment of the ten which deals with time is the fourth, the one that identifies God as the ruler of time by the fact that after He had created the world He created the Sabbath. It was this precept concerning which Daniel predicted an attempted change in God's law.

Most readers of these lines know that this prediction has found its fulfillment in history!

A Last-Day Message of Reform

In time's last hour world attention is to be called once again to the Sabbath of the Creator and to the Creator of the Sabbath. Revelation 14:6, 7, speaks of a message which is to ring out to "every nation, and kindred, and tongue, and people, saying with a loud voice, Fear God, and give glory to him; for the hour of his judgment is come: and worship him that made heaven, and earth, and the sea, and the fountains of waters." These words are too similar to the words of the Sabbath commandment to be accidental:

"Remember . . . the sabbath of the Lord thy God . . . [who] made heaven and earth, the sea, and all that in them is." Exodus 20:8-11.

It is impossible to proclaim the Creator of the Sabbath without proclaiming the Sabbath of the Creator. The two are inseparably linked. Then, as the prophet looks for the group who have been separated from error and disobedience by the proclamation of this message, he exclaims, "Here are they!" "Here are they that keep the commandments of God, and the faith of Jesus." Revelation 14:12. He sees a group of people who in time's last hour, just before Jesus comes (see verse 14), are keeping all the commandments of God, including the fourth, which says, "Remember . . . the sabbath of the Lord thy God." Exodus 20:8-10.

These people are keeping, not the sun festival of the pagans, not the pseudo-sabbath handed down to Christendom by human tradition without any vestige of biblical authority; they are keeping the Sabbath of the Lord their God. This prophecy has been wonderfully fulfilled in our day. Throughout the length and breadth of earth, on every continent these Sabbath-keeping Christians are to be found. They believe that Jesus is coming soon. They're preparing for the day when "it shall come to pass, that . . . from one sabbath to another, shall all flesh come to worship before me, saith the Lord." Isaiah 66:23.

Revelation 14:12 identifies these people as "the saints" (the holy ones), those whose lives are characterized by loyalty to God in an era of universal apostasy. In Revelation, chapter 13, you have the high-water mark of apostasy—the entire world wondering after (that is, giving their allegiance to) the beast. By contrast, Revelation 12 is the high-water mark of loyalty—a small group of people, swimming upstream in defiance of popular practice. The saints. The holy ones. The loyal ones. Those who give their allegiance to God. Those who are prepared to go all the way with Jesus.

A Day of Worship

"Remember the sabbath day, to keep it holy. Six days shalt thou labour, and do all thy work: but the seventh day is the sabbath of the Lord thy God." Exodus 20:8-10.

A careful reading of this commandment reveals that it does not merely make provision for "one day in seven" to be spent sunbathing, fishing, gardening, golfing, or in some other form of sport or relaxation. Important as time for relaxation may be, this is not the purpose or function of the Sabbath. The whole idea of the Sabbath is to take our thoughts off ourselves and our own pursuits and to focus them on God! God is saying in effect, "I have given you six days to devote to your personal, secular pursuits, but the seventh day, the Sabbath, belongs to Me! On that day I require you to lay aside your own pursuits and devote your attention to the God who has made it possible for you to have life and who has provided everything you need to maintain life. The very strength and faculties you need to pursue your vocation and earn your daily bread you get from Me. Now all I ask is that you devote this one day to worshiping Me."

The precise wording of the Sabbath commandment leaves no room for anyone to doubt as to what God had in mind in instituting it for His people. He commands us to "keep it," not merely to "spend it." He instructs us to "keep it holy," not merely to cease from labor. He calls it "the sabbath of the Lord thy God," not a "rest day" on which we can elect to do as we please. It is His day, not ours. We are to observe His day as He wills, not as we please!

"If thou turn away thy foot from the sabbath, from doing thy pleasure on my holy day; and call the sabbath a delight, the holy of the Lord, honourable; and shalt honour him, not doing thine own ways, nor finding thine own pleasure, nor speaking thine own words: then shalt thou delight thyself in the Lord; and I will cause thee to ride upon the high places of the earth, and feed thee with the heritage of Jacob thy father: for the mouth of the Lord hath spoken it." Isaiah 58:13, 14.

"God has given men six days wherein to labor, and He requires that their own work be done in the six working days. Acts of necessity and mercy are permitted on the Sabbath, the sick and suffering are at all times to be cared for; but unnecessary labor is to be strictly avoided. 'Turn away thy foot from the Sabbath, from doing thy pleasure on My holy day; and call the Sabbath a delight, the holy of the Lord, honourable; and . . . honour Him, not doing thine own ways, nor finding thine own pleasure.' Isaiah 58:13.

Nor does the prohibition end here. 'Nor speaking thine own words,' says the prophet. Those who discuss business matters or lay plans on the Sabbath are regarded by God as though engaged in the actual transaction of business. To keep the Sabbath holy, we should not even allow our minds to dwell upon things of a worldly character. And the commandment includes all within our gates. The inmates of the house are to lay aside their worldly business during the sacred hours. All should unite to honor God by willing service upon His holy day."—*Patriarchs and Prophets*, pp. 307, 308.

A Sign of Sanctification

God declares the Sabbath to be a sign between Himself and His people. He declares it to be a sign of sanctification. See Ezekiel 20:12, 20 and Exodus 31:12-18.

How does the Sabbath become an agency of sanctification? By virtue of the fact that it is by God's power that we are sanctified, or made holy (see Romans 15:16; Jude 1; 1 Thessalonians 5:23, 24), and the Sabbath is designed to expose our souls to His sanctifying power.

Furthermore, the Bible declares that we are sanctified by the truth. John 17:17. By keeping holy the day which God ordained it be kept holy, we identify ourselves with Him who is truth (John 14:6), with the teachings of His Word, which is truth (John 17:17), and with the sacred claims of His law, which is truth (Psalm 119:142).

"This is the will of God, even your sanctification." 1 Thessalonians 4:3. This is the Sabbath's real function—to serve as a means of contributing to our sanctification! A holy God uses a holy day to make a holy people! It is His design that on His holy day His people shall expose themselves to every influence that can contribute to making them a little bit more holy: studying His holy Word, worshiping in His holy place, worshiping the Holy God, revering His holy name, enjoying fellowship with the holy angels, sitting at the crucified feet of their holy Saviour, and being convicted of sin, righteousness, and judgment by the Holy Spirit. A holy day, a holy people—inseparably linked. The first an integral part of God's plan for the accomplishment of the second. God designs that next Sabbath, and each Sabbath of your life until He comes, shall leave you a little bit more holy than it found you; shall draw you closer to Himself; shall lead you onto higher ground; shall be a vital factor in your sanctification, which is His ultimate goal for your life.

Chapter VII

God's design when He created the human race was that people would live together in family circles, composed of a father, who would be the head and priest of the family and provide for its material needs; a mother, who would provide tender loving care for her family; and children, who would look up to their parents for instruction, guidance, direction, and protection as they themselves prepared to take their place as members of society. He intended that the home would be the seedbed in which children would grow into noble manhood and womanhood.

The fifth commandment, "Honour thy father and mother," makes it clear that in God's scheme of things there were to be two parents and that they were meant to be equals in the partnership of parenthood. Both are mentioned in the commandment as being worthy of honor. Children were intended to grow up happy in the security that belonging to a family circle brings.

God's interest in youth is shown by the fact that in the midst of His law He has placed a commandment that directly affects their spiritual and temporal welfare. Young people must be very near to the heart of God for Him to have addressed them in the heart of His holy law!

Some fifteen times in the first seven chapters of Proverbs, the words "my son" occur. Five of these first seven chapters open with the words "My son." This surely tells us something about the tender solicitude God has for his earthly children and about the importance He attaches to the father-to-son and son-to-father relationship!

It is significant that the commandment dealing with child-parent relationships is placed immediately next to the Sabbath commandment. This sequence is not accidental. The fourth commandment identifies God as the Creator and safeguards His authority. The fifth commandment safeguards the parental authority of those who, under God, have given life to their offspring.

It is also significant that the commandment that has to do with home relationships precedes the commandments that forbid murder, adultery, stealing, and lying. These are sins of society, and the nucleus of society is the home. So God is trying to tell us that the place to begin dealing with the ills of society is in the home! Teach a child to honor his parents, to respect their authority, to render them obedience, and to cherish principles of unselfishness, morality, honesty, and truthfulness within the home circle, and that child will automatically put those principles into practice when he leaves the family circle to take his place in society.

Prison records reveal that criminals generally are not people who have had sound home training as children. More often than not they are persons who knew nothing of parental restraint or discipline in childhood and youth. As a result they became transgressors of the fifth commandment, and this in time led them to violate the sixth, seventh, eighth, and ninth commandments. Their renunciation of parental authority opened the door onto the road of disregard for the laws of God and of society.

There are, of course, some notable exceptions to this rule. We know of cases where children from exemplary homes have grown up to live lives of recklessness, licentiousness, dishonesty, and deception. They did not learn these things in their homes. In some cases they were taught by evil companions. In certain other cases the fault lay with the schools they attended. Only too often the damage was done by pernicious literature. We are here dealing, however, with the rule. That rule is unmistakably stated in God's law: *The home is the tree-nursery* of society. Cultivate the plant carefully there, and the tree will be healthy when it takes root in the outside world.

Notice further that the commandment which says, "Honour thy father and thy mother," forms a bridge between those precepts of the law which deal with our duty to God and those which deal with our duty to our fellowmen. The first four commandments define our duty to God, the last six our duty to our fellows. The fulcrum which balances these two portions of the law is the fifth commandment. When a child learns in his home to love and obey God, he will express that love for God by loving his fellowmen. On the other hand, the way to teach a child to honor God is to teach him to honor his parents. A child's parents are his first representation of God. Before his mind is capable of comprehending God, his parents are to him a personification of God through whom he is to learn to know the invisible and eternal heavenly Father. Their authority is to take the place of the authority of God during the formative years of life before the developing mind can grasp the significance of God's requirements. A small child cannot be taught what it means to obey God. But he can be taught what it means to obey! Gradually this principle of obedience will unfold in his life to embrace the realization that his obedience to his earthly parents was but an elementary expression of a higher loyalty to his unseen Parent.

It isn't difficult to understand why lawlessness, iniquity, and crime abound in our age, is it? Because the foundations of the home have crumbled, moral decay has set in at every level of society. The cure does not lie in penal measures against crime but in a revival of home religion. We are not saying that punishment of crime is unnecessary in a sick society. It is assuredly needed. But it can never effect a cure. It can accomplish no more than to arrest the spread of the disease to a limited extent. The cure must begin at the heart of society—in the home.

What does it mean to "honour thy father and thy mother"? The word *honour* was carefully chosen by God in connection with this command. He might have said "love" or "obey." He purposely used the word He did. "Love" might have implied a sentimental relationship. "Honour" is not merely sentimental or emotional. It calls for an exercise of the intellect and the will. It implies an active, not a passive, regard. It means giving them the deference which their parental office merits, regardless of whether or not we happen to "like" them! Sometimes children are heard to say that they find it difficult to like their parents because of dispositional defects in their lives. This is, however, no excuse for them not to honor them. They are still their parents, their undesirable traits of character notwithstanding.

Likewise, the word *obey* might have implied a blind obedience, which exacting parents might have used as a basis for making unreasonable demands on their children. To honor involves obeying in all matters which are not contrary to God's will. This is made clear in the New Testament where we are told, "Children, obey your parents in the Lord." Ephesians 6:1. When a parent requires a child to do anything that is contrary to God's revealed will, he exceeds his prerogatives as a trustee and forfeits the right to be obeyed. But when a parent's requirements *are* in harmony with God's requirements, it is the duty of a child to obey. To obey his parents, then, involves obeying God.

Honoring our parents means giving them the respect they deserve. It involves honoring their wishes. It will reveal itself in an interest in their welfare and happiness. In this respect Jesus has set young people a supreme example. When hanging in agony on the cross, His heart reached out in tender pity to His mother, and He committed her to the care of one of His most trustworthy disciples. In honoring their parents, children are following in the footsteps of Jesus!

Honoring our parents means as well that we will strive never to bring dishonor on the family name. Sometimes friends will tempt unwary youth to participate in certain activities secretly and surreptitiously so that their parents will not know about these contacts. Teenage girls will be asked by boys of their age-group, or by older men, to keep dates about which their parents know nothing. Such youth can be sure that the motives of those who make such suggestions are invariably dishonorable. Young people would spare themselves many a headache and heartache if they would adopt as their motto in life, "If my parents can't know, why should I do it?" It stands to reason that sensible parents desire only the immediate and ultimate happiness of their children. It therefore follows that they would not want to deny them any real pleasure unless they knew that it would result in injury to them. The simple fact is that young people who resent so-called "parental interference" and "parental restraint" do so because, in the foolishness of their young hearts, they think they know better, or even that they know everything! This is really nothing other than a species of idolatry—of sinful pride and self-worship. It is from this form of idolatry, with its attendant snares and pitfalls, that God so graciously seeks to deliver us by placing the command "Honour thy father and thy mother" in the heart of His law.

Those who heed this injunction not only render obedience to a divine requirement, but save themselves from many soul- and body-destroying evils that beset the path of unsuspecting youth. That is why God finishes this command with a promise—"that thy days may be long upon the land which the Lord thy God giveth thee." There's nothing magical about this blessing! God is but stating the simple fact that the youth who obey His fifth command are thereby saved from the evils that destroy their disobedient fellows. Their "days" are "long" both with respect to the present life and the life to come. "With long life [this present life] will I satisfy him, and shew him my salvation [the life to come]." Psalm 91:16.

Another way in which we honor our parents is to honor their memory after their death. This we do by living lives that are worthy of that memory. A person dishonors his parents who, either during their lifetime or after their death, brings shame upon their name. One who honors his father and his mother will ever strive to live a life that will fill their hearts with pride and satisfaction while they live, and that will be a memorial to their sacrifices and training when they are gone.

The Elijah Message

The Old Testament closes with a most significant prophecy: "Behold, I will send you Elijah the prophet before the coming of the great and dreadful day of the Lord: and he shall turn the heart of the fathers to the children, and the heart of the children to their fathers." Malachi 4:5, 6. The prophet here described a special message of reform which is to be proclaimed "before the coming of the great and dreadful day of the Lord." It is described as the Elijah message.

Elijah's special role was to call attention to the requirements of God's law. "Ye have forsaken the commandments of the Lord, and thou hast followed Baalim." "How long halt ye between two opinions? if the Lord be God, follow him: but if Baal, then follow him." 1 Kings 18:18, 21. Once again, in time's last hour, this message is to ring out to earth's remotest bounds, calling the world back to obedience to God's law.

The prophet Malachi especially emphasizes the universal disregard of the fifth commandment. The apostle Paul likewise portrays this condition: "This know also, that in the last days perilous times shall come. For men shall be . . . *disobedient to parents . . . , without natural affection*." 2 Timothy 3:1-3. On the part of children, lack of obedience to their parents; on the part of parents, lack of affection for their children—this would be the spiritual and social climate of "the last days." How remarkably this prediction is being fulfilled in our day! Indeed the breakdown of the family unit is one of the most notable signs of the times.

Not only is disobedience to parents specifically listed in this catalog of conditions that will characterize the last days, but the other items listed are, by and large, social ills that stem directly from the breakdown of the home and the dissolution of the family! Notice what Paul says in Romans 1:28-30—disobedience to parents is itemized as one of the marks of apostasy and rebellion against God.

Another aspect of Elijah's prophetic role was that he restored the altar that had been broken down. 1 Kings 18:30. This phase of his ministry is also to find its fulfillment in the last-day reformatory movement which bears his name. Parents would have fewer problems in getting their children to honor them, if their children knew that the parents honored their heavenly Father. They can give their children evidence of this fact by meeting together regularly and consistently around the family altar!

The prophet Malachi foretells that one of the results of the preaching of the Elijah message—a message that exalts the law of God—is that fathers will love their children and children will obey their fathers, representing a complete reversal of a trend!

By authority of the inspired Word we affirm the fulfillment of this precious promise to all who with sincere hearts will seek God's grace to fulfill this and the other requirements of God's great standard of right living. With His help, obey Him. Give Him the chance to fulfill His promise to you and to your family.

Chapter VIII

Possibly fewer people stand condemned as transgressors of the sixth commandment than any of the others, if we go by the letter of the law, that is. The commandment consists of four short words: "Thou shalt not kill." However, the law of God reaches down into our thoughts and motives. It touches the innermost intents and feelings of our hearts. It weighs not only our deeds but our words. It measures not only our conduct but our character, not only our behavior but our spirit.

It is possible, says God's Word, for a man never to be condemned as a murderer in court, and yet be a murderer in his heart! "Whosoever hateth his brother is a murderer; and ye know that no murderer hath eternal life abiding in him." 1 John 3:15.

When we allow our souls to cherish feelings of hatred against someone, those murderous feelings are recorded against us as murder. When we come to hate an individual so much that we find ourselves saying in our hearts, "I wish he were dead," that desire is reckoned as though we had accomplished his death.

"But," you say, "it is only my brother that I am commanded not to hate. That's easy! I love my 'brethren.' But there is nothing in this passage that forbids my hating my enemies. I love all those who love God. But those who hate God and who despise His holy name I hate!" What of this? Let us ask Jesus the question. "Ye have heard that it hath been said, Thou shalt love thy neighbour, and hate thine enemy. But I say unto you, Love your enemies, bless them that curse you, do good to them that hate you, and pray for them which despitefully use you, and persecute you; that ye may be the children of your Father which is in heaven: for he maketh his sun to rise on the evil and on the good, and sendeth rain on the just and on the unjust. For if ye love them which love you, what reward have ye? do not even the publicans the same? And if ye salute your brethren only, what do ye more than others? do not even the publicans so? Be ye therefore perfect, even as your Father which is in heaven is perfect." Matthew 5:43-48.

Do you see from this statement that it is our love for our enemies that is the very test of our religion? Jesus says if we love only those who are our "brethren" we are no different from the pagans. They are also capable of loving the members of their own fraternity, but their love does not embrace those who lie outside those boundaries. The evidence of our Christianity is the very fact that our love is able to transcend these boundaries and reach out to include even our enemies!

This is all very well in theory. But when it comes to interpreting it into the practical aspects of daily living, it is an altogether different matter! A drunken driver kills my child on the road. What is my wish for that man? That he be locked up? Or that he learn to flee for refuge to the Saviour instead of to the bottle? We are dealing with the heart of religion.

We have some magnificent examples in history of how, when God moves in, the spirit of hatred and revenge is replaced with that of love and reconciliation. This is the ultimate evidence that there is a God in the universe. The tendency to love those who have done us harm is not a human tendency. When love for our enemies prevails in our lives over our natural inclination to hate them, it is unmistakable evidence that God is at work in these hearts of ours!

I witnessed a heartwarming evidence of God's power to accomplish this when I had the privilege of visiting Coventry Cathedral a couple of years ago. No visitor to Britain should miss Coventry Cathedral. It will do something to your soul that cannot be explained in human terms. You will never be the same person again. The old cathedral was almost totally destroyed by the German Luftwaffe during World War II. The shell of the once beautiful medieval structure stands next to the new cathedral as a stark monument to the ravages of war. In the lovely new edifice is a magnificent window—a gift from the people of Dresden, Germany! Now the thing that makes this gift so magnificent is that Dresden was almost totally destroyed by the R.A.F. during the same war in which the Luftwaffe nearly destroyed Coventry. Underneath the window appears an inscription that cannot fail to bring tears to one's eyes and a lump to one's throat. In English the simple prayer "God forgive Dresden" and next to it in German "God forgive Coventry." This is the spirit of Christianity. This is the spirit of Calvary. This is the spirit of Christianity. This is the spirit of Calvary. This is the spirit of the Master who prayed on the cross, "Father, forgive them."

In her book *The Hiding Place*, Corrie ten Boom tells of her encounter with one of her captors during the wartime occupation of Holland by that country's invaders.

"It was at a church service in Munich that I saw him, the former S.S. man who had stood guard at the shower room door in the processing center at Ravensbruck. He was the first of our actual jailers that I had seen since that time. And suddenly it was all there—the roomful of mocking men, the heaps of clothing, Betsie's pain-blanched face.

"He came up to me as the church was emptying, beaming and bowing. 'How grateful I am for your message *Fräulein,*' he said. 'To think that, as you say, He has washed my sins away!'

"His hand was thrust out to shake mine. And I, who had preached so often to the people in Bloemendal the need to forgive, kept my hand at my side.

"Even as the angry, vengeful thoughts boiled through me, I saw the sin of them. Jesus Christ had died for this man; was I going to ask for more? Lord Jesus, I prayed, forgive me and help me to forgive him.

"I tried to smile, I struggled to raise my hand. I could not. I felt nothing, not the slightest spark of warmth or charity. And so again I breathed a silent prayer. Jesus, I cannot forgive him. Give me your forgiveness.

"As I took his hand the most incredible thing happened. From my shoulder along my arm and through my hand a current seemed to pass from me to him, while into my heart sprang a love for this stranger that almost overwhelmed me.

"And so I discovered that it is not on our forgiveness any more than on our goodness that the world's healing hinges, but on His. When He tells us to love our enemies, He gives, along with the command, the love itself."[10]

"The love of God is something more than a mere negation; it is a positive and active principle, a living spring, ever flowing to bless others. If the love of Christ dwells in us, we shall not only cherish no hatred toward our fellows, but we shall seek in every way to manifest love toward them."—*Thoughts From the Mount of Blessing*, p. 58.

Gentleness

The precious gem of gentleness is given extremely high value in the Word of God. The apostle Paul says, "And the servant of the Lord must not strive; but be gentle unto all men, apt to teach, patient." 2 Timothy 2:24. We are told that God's gentleness gives greatness, or quality, to the character. See 2 Samuel 22:36; Psalm 18:35. Gentleness is listed as one of the fruits of the Spirit in the life of the reborn Christian. See Galatians 5:22. This Christian quality is asked for again and again in the letters to the members of the early church. See Titus 3:2; James 3:17; 2 Corinthians 10:1. Kindness, a twin sister of gentleness, is listed as the second to last rung of the ladder of Christian perfection set forth in 2 Peter 1:7—preceded by godliness and followed by the crowning virtue of charity.

At an hour in their history when the Jews were looking for a deliverer who would break the yoke of Roman bondage from off their necks and when hatred for their oppressors had reached its high-water mark, along came a young Galilean who startled them with the revolutionary new doctrine of nonviolence and gentleness, which He not only preached but practiced! Consider these samples of the Saviour's gentleness at a time when toughness was what His compatriots wanted:

His healing of a Roman centurion's servant. Matthew 8:5-10.

His restoration of Malchus's ear in the Garden of Gethsemane. Luke 22:49-51. Cf. John 18:10.

His prayer for His persecutors as He hung on the cross. Luke 23:34.

His solicitude for the spiritual need of the criminal hanging on the cross next to His. Luke 23:42, 43.

His solicitude for His mother in the hour of His own intense suffering. John 19:26, 27.

His regard for Peter in the face of his shameful denial of his Master. John 21:15-17.

His concern for the multitude who were hungry after listening to Him all day. Matthew 14:15-20.

His concern for the rich young ruler who asked Him the way of salvation. Luke 18:18-24.

His interest in Zacchaeus, a hated tax collector. Luke 19:5-10.

His concern for the woman accused of being an adultress. John 8:3-11.

His interest in a Samaritan at Jacob's well. John 4:6-30.

The Question of War

A truly vexing question is that of war. The question is so complex that to try and deal with it is simply to get into a labyrinth. The problem could be debated till the end of time without a definitive answer being found. One side would argue with great earnestness that Christ declared, "Put up thy sword." "My kingdom is not of this world: if my kingdom were of this world, then would my servants fight." John 18:11, 36. The other side would argue with equal sincerity that God commanded ancient Israel to destroy their godless enemies and that godless forces and ideologies are abroad in the world today which must also be dealt with. It is also one's duty, these folks would forcibly argue, to defend one's home, one's family, and one's country, if and when attacked. These are valid arguments. But when they have been cited, the last word has by no means been said.

To the born-again child of God, who, while recognizing his duty to his country, truly feels that his citizenship is in the kingdom of God, war is something altogether at variance with his spiritual experience. He recognizes that all too often wars are not the holy crusades they profess to be, but are mere political games of chess in which human life is of less value than the gains of war. He cannot escape the personal moral accountability of terminating the earthly life of someone whom he knows is, in all probability, not prepared to stand before the judgment seat of God and who, had he lived, might eventually have been. He also faces the dilemma of possibly being called on to fight against someone who, although wearing the uniform of the enemy, may well be a brother of his in Christ. All these knotty factors force themselves upon us when dealing with the problem of war.

There is only one commonsense approach to the question, as we see it. In so delicate an issue, no one can be conscience for another. Every man is personally accountable to God. No one can dictate to another how he should relate himself to this accountability. Fortunately for those who have conscientious convictions on the matter of combatant service in time of war, provision is made in many countries whereby these persons can serve their country and their fellowmen in noncombatant capacities. We honor world leaders that make these provisions possible. We pray that God will give them grace and wisdom as they strive for the well-being of the world and all its people. We assure them that they will find those who do not see their way clear to take up guns to be nevertheless stalwart and loyal supporters on whom they can rely in times of crisis.

"My Brother's Keeper"

Are we not guilty of transgressing the sixth commandment when we allow someone to die whose life it was in our power to save? Would it be saying too much if we said that it is the duty of every Christian to know how to render emergency aid when it is needed, lest the flickering flame of life be snuffed out when help at the right time could have prevented it? Right here we are constrained to pay tribute to the marvel of blood transfusion which has saved untold thousands of lives that would have ended before the advent of this lifesaving agency. Yet there are those who believe that blood transfusion is sinful.

We have actually read of cases where persons of that persuasion have been prepared to stand by and see one of their children die, when the child's life could have been saved by a blood transfusion. We cannot help wondering whether the sin was not in thus allowing someone to die who could have lived. We know of no valid Bible principle that is violated by so doing. Our aim should ever be to save life, never to lose it. This, surely, is the spirit of the sixth commandment and of the gospel which endorses it.

Suicide

Suicide is another aspect of the subject we need to consider briefly. The Christian church has always regarded the termination of one's own life to be as much a violation of the sixth commandment as taking the life of someone else. This does not give us the right to pass judgment on anyone who has terminated his own life. Nor do we have the right to assume that such a person is beyond hope. God alone knows the full circumstances of each case and understands the deep desperation that would lead a person to take so drastic a step. We can rejoice that God is the judge and that He will judge every case justly and fairly. It nevertheless behooves us to state the church's position unequivocally as being opposed to suicide, just as it is to any form of murder. Whenever it occurs within our church-family circle, however, we need rather than pass judgment, to search our hearts and ascertain whether any neglect on our part could have contributed to, or whether any act or word of encouragement on our part could have averted the tragedy.

Having laid down the principle that the church views with disfavor, though with compassion, the termination of one's own life under any circumstance, we could well take a look at some pertinent questions. What would you say, then, about acts which tend to end one's life, not all at once, but by degrees? Suppose, for instance, a man took very small doses of arsenic daily—not enough to kill him outright, but enough so that it would kill him off slowly over a period of time? Now let's make our point: Dr. Alton Ochsner, the illustrious former president of the American College of Surgeons, has established by means of a very thorough study of the subject, that each cigarette smoked shortens life by 14.4 minutes. A fifty year-old person who has never smoked will live an average of eight and a half years longer than a person who smokes a pack a day, and seventeen years longer than one who smokes two packs a day.

The liquor traffic also comes under condemnation when we deal with the sixth commandment. When it can be proved by irrefutable evidence that liquor causes the death of hundreds of thousands every year—through highway and industrial accidents, through suicides brought about by the despair and weariness of life that liquor induces, through the neglect of children that it causes, through liver and other organic diseases that it inflicts, through many other direct and indirect causes too numerous to mention—then how, we ask, can those who ply this evil trade and who tolerate it for mercenary gain stand clear before God? Will the veritable tide of human life squandered in the plying of this demonic traffic not be required of them?

The sixth commandment is a deep-searching X ray that searches out in the deepest recesses of our souls every trace of the cancer of selfishness and hate. It exposes it to the searching eye of Him who said, "I am come that they might have life, and that they might have it more abundantly." John 10:10. It is our happy privilege not only to enjoy this life ourselves, but to ensure that others will enjoy it with us and because of us!

Abortion

Another extremely sensitive area, which we cannot avoid looking at in considering the sixth commandment, is that of abortion. Abortion unquestionably involves the termination of human life, and the church views with disfavor the termination of human life. Having laid down this principle, let us hasten to add that we should look at the situation with compassion. Whenever the mother of an unborn child opts for this route out of a dilemma, for whatever reason, there is a work of healing that needs to be done. The church has no right to wrap itself in a shroud of self-righteous indifference in such cases. The church's hands should be the very first, and the very warmest, to be stretched out in healing. Once again the question would be well worth pondering: Did failure on our part—to instruct, to guide, to protect—result in the tragedy? Could the correct groundwork have averted the tragedy before it occurred?

Chapter IX

"I would like to request your kind advice in the following matter," wrote a young lady not known to me personally. "Can you please give me biblical evidence that it is wrong for two people to live together without being married. My friend and I have been living together for two weeks now. I cannot escape the feeling that it is wrong, but I do not have biblical proof. My partner believes that it is not wrong in God's eyes if two people love each other. He was baptized a month ago, and I would like to be baptized as soon as I know that my life is right with the Lord. I feel that I must either be fully for the Lord, or not for Him at all. This problem is one of the things that is standing between myself and a full surrender of my life to God."

What does one say to a young person who asks a question like that? Would I have been helping her if I had given this answer? "Well, after all, you're lonely. God understands your circumstances. So don't let it bother you. What you're doing isn't really all that bad, under your circumstances."

Here is what I told her. I have her permission to share her letter and my reply with you for the benefit of others who may have a similar problem.

"The thing that makes 'living together' *wrong*, and marriage *right*, is the respective foundations on which the two life-styles rest. 'Living together' rests on the foundation of the understanding that at any time the relationship could end. As soon as one or the other of the partners gets tired of the other or they decide mutually that they're tired of each other, they can part. There is no fusion of two lives as one. The two do not *belong* to each other.

"In marriage, on the other hand, there is a foundation of *belonging* to each other in a permanent, irrevocable life-partnership. It's like two rivers that flow into each other to become one. Their waters now intermingle with each other so completely that it's no longer possible to distinguish one from the other.

"The Bible makes it very clear that this is the nature of marriage, and the order of marriage intended by God. Read Ephesians 5:23-33 and notice particularly verse 31, which makes it clear that when a man is joined to his wife, they become *one*. There can be absolutely no doubt that this is the divine order of marriage. Anything outside of this order is thus outside of God's plan, and hence is sin.

" 'Living together' just *cannot* ever measure up to this divine plan because there is no permanence built into the foundation—no sense of *belonging* to each other for life, which is what marriage is all about!

"Let me state very clearly that the reason why you are unhappy about your relationship is that *it is God* who is telling you that it is wrong! Either you should get married to the man with whom you are living and become his for life, or you should break off your relationship and come to the parting of your ways. *There is no third alternative*. It must be one or the other. God has already told you which one it should be. You cannot reject or refuse what God's voice is saying to you except at the peril of your soul!

"God bless you as you follow His instruction. To do so will contribute toward your present happiness and your eternal salvation. To refuse to do so will result only in misery now and the loss of your soul hereafter. I pray you will make the right choice."

It came as a considerable relief when she wrote back to say, "Thank you very much for your letter and for the advice therein. I understand the matter very clearly now, as you have explained it very well and I have no more questions on this matter. I have good news for you today. I broke off this wrong relationship on New Year's Eve. There was a lot of unpleasantness at the time, but I thank the Lord that He has helped me to sort out this matter, as it was worrying me very much."

Has she taken a backward step psychologically? On the contrary. Each subsequent letter reveals a slow but steady growth in her life of discipleship and fellowship with Christ and the joy and fulfillment she is experiencing in that relationship. She is discovering a richness and fullness in life that a life-style out of harmony with God's revealed will could never give her.

An isolated instance? We think not. It illustrates that the permissive attitude of society toward sex and marriage is knocking at the door of the church. If we refuse or neglect to come to grips with this fact, it will be at the peril of our homes and of the souls of those who reside in them. When the world's criterion is accepted by church members, as it obviously had been in the case of the young man referred to in the letter, we can get some inkling of the extent to which this humanistic philosophy has pervaded society at large!

For a long time we have known that powerful forces have been at work in our world that are bent on destroying the institutions of marriage and the home, and that would reduce what was designed to be a permanent and precious partnership to the level of a temporary mating process serving nothing but a sexually functional role.

Karl Marx, in his historic *Communist Manifesto*, made this declaration: "The proletarian revolution will establish the socialist dictatorship of the proletariat. But before this can happen three important things must be accomplished: first, the elimination of all right to private property; second, the dissolution of the family unit; third, the destruction of religion, 'the opiate of the people.' "

The humanist Aldous Huxley in his provocative book *Brave New World* suggests that "in a few years, no doubt, marriage licenses will be sold like dog licenses, good for a period of twelve months, with no law against changing dogs or keeping more than one animal at a time."

The onslaught against marriage didn't begin, however, with Marx or Huxley. They are but echoing the sentiments of many others in past ages who have supposed they could improve on God's plan. We can trace the story of the struggle to destroy the home down through the civilizations of Rome and Greece (with similar results to what we are witnessing today—the dissolution of civilization), and further back than that to the nations that surrounded God's Old Testament nation-church Israel—nations whose sexual perversion brought upon them God's destruction. See Leviticus 18:3-30. It was against the contamination of their sensual philosophy that God needed constantly to warn His people and which represented an unrelenting threat to their spiritual life.

We can trace the story of the struggle back even further to Sodom and Gomorrah. These cities were visited by God in judgment for their immoral way of life. See Genesis 19:4-9. Will a just God countenance in modern society that for which He punished society in days of old?

But we can go back even further than that, to the very gates of the Garden of Eden! It is interesting to note how rapidly society plunged into degradation once man rejected God's sovereignty! In Genesis, chapter 3, we have the story of the Fall, and in chapter 4—the very next chapter!—we find the record of the first two murders (see Genesis 4:8, 23) and of man's first departure from God's plan for marriage, namely, the first recorded instance of bigamy (see Genesis 4:19).

The Church's Responsibility

The one bulwark that remains to confront these destructive forces and to stand in defense of the home and the institution of marriage is the church. What are its grounds for supporting what many regard as an archaic and old-fashioned institution?

First of all, marriage rests on the fact that man is a unique order of being, the masterpiece of a divine Designer and Creator. Man is not a creature of chance. Man is not a modified version of the ape. Man was created by God and for God and in the moral image of God. Saint Augustine was speaking the truth when he said, "God made us for Himself, and our souls can find no rest until they find their rest in Him."

Second, the Master Designer who made us, ordained that we should live together as family units, each comprising one man, one woman, and, normally, children who would develop their highest physical, intellectual, social, and spiritual capabilities in the framework of an atmosphere in which they would enjoy the security born out of the sense of belonging to that couple and of that couple belonging to each other.

This is what marriage is all about. Belonging. Belonging to each other. The function of marriage is belonging. When a married couple come together in love, they are saying to each other, "I belong to you; you belong to me; in a special sense, a unique sense, an exclusive sense, we belong to each other—inseparably, irrevocably." This is God's way. This is the divine order, the order ordained for us by the Master Craftsman who designed and made us!

This relationship between partners in marriage of belonging to each other in a special, unique, exclusive sense is used in Scripture to symbolize the mystical relationship between Christ and His church. Christ, the husband, gives Himself in love to His wife; and Christ's bride, the church, is to respond to His love just as a woman in the marriage relationship responds to her husband's love.

These are the immovable pillars on which the institution of marriage rests. These are the irrefutable facts that make marriage unchangeably and unchangingly relevant.

This being true, it stands to reason that any deviation from God's intended plan for marriage—whether that deviation be premarital sex, homosexuality, adultery, fornication, "living together," bigamy, or polygamy—is a deviation from His design, and hence from His will, and thus constitutes sin. And, since it is impossible to defy divine law without suffering the consequences, it is inevitable that any such deviation from the design of the Designer with reference to marriage must bring in its train dire consequences to the individual and to society as a whole.

We are today witnessing the results and are reaping the harvest of the world's disregard of God's law as it relates to the sacredness of sex: a harvest of the total dissolution of moral values. The only thing left on earth to check this moral rottenness is the church. And if the attitudes that pervade society invade the church or slowly erode its defenses, all is lost. Through the church God is making a last-ditch stand against the assault of the enemy in which his takeover of society is well-nigh complete.

In our modern climate of permissiveness, many people would regard the church's attitude toward sexual perversion as harsh and judgmental. Is it being harsh and judgmental to say that electricity, which is a power for good when harnessed and channeled, is deadly dangerous and destructive when it is not carefully controlled? Even so with sexual relationships.

The work that has been committed to us is a work of reform, and in no area is reform more urgently needed than in that relating to our homes. "We are to labor to restore to men and women the sense of moral obligation which has been lost."—*This Day With God*, p. 71. "Marriage has been perverted by sin; but it is the purpose of the gospel to restore its purity and beauty."—*Thoughts From the Mount of Blessing*, p. 64.

The Testimony of Scripture

The Bible neither ignores nor condemns the fact of human sexuality. Christianity does not identify itself with religious philosophies that regard "the flesh," and everything associated with it, as sinful. It recognizes sexual desire as a normal drive built into the physiological and psychological makeup of human beings by the Creator Himself.

Christianity condemns as sinful only those manifestations of "the flesh" that are outside of God's purpose and design. It avoids either of two extremes—celibacy as the path to holiness, and acceptance of *all forms* of sexual expression as being essentially normal and proper. The scriptural view, and hence the Christian church's view, of sexual experience is that it is exclusive to a relationship between one man and one woman who belong to each other in a total lifelong commitment. It is the bonding agency infusing a husband and wife into a permanent partnership.

Concerning the seventh commandment, the Bible has more to say than on any of the other commandments. Practically every Bible writer bears testimony to the sinfulness of sexual experience outside of marriage. The sum total of their combined testimony is that there is no sin which is more displeasing to God than this. Says the apostle Paul: "Now the works of the flesh are manifest, which are these; Adultery, fornication, uncleanness, lasciviousness . . . : they which do such things shall not inherit the kingdom of God." Galatians 5:19-21.

His message is equally pointed to the Thessalonians, especially as paraphrased by J. B. Phillips. "God's plan is to make you holy, and *that entails first of all a clean cut with sexual immorality*. Every one of you should learn to control his body, keeping it pure and treating it with respect, and never regarding it as an instrument for self-gratification, as do pagans with no knowledge of God. You cannot break this rule without in some way cheating your fellow men. And you must remember that God will punish all who do offend in this matter, and we have warned you how we have seen this work out in our experience of life. *The calling of God is not to impurity but to the most thorough purity*, and anyone who makes light of the matter is not making light of a man's ruling but of God's command. *It is not for nothing that the Spirit God gives us is called the Holy Spirit*." 1 Thessalonians 4:3-8. Emphasis supplied. See also Ephesians 5:3, 5; Colossians 3:5, 6; and Revelation 22:15.

The Old Testament writers were equally explicit in their denunciation of this evil. Wrote Malachi: "I will come near to you to judgment; and I will be a swift witness . . . against the adulterers, . . . saith the Lord of hosts." Malachi 3:5. Isaiah, Jeremiah, Ezekiel, Hosea, and Amos bear testimony in similarly explicit language. The law of Moses condemned a long list of sexual perversions. See Leviticus 18:20, 22-27, 29, 30 and 20:7, 10-12, 14-17, 20-23. One expression that frequently accompanies these scriptural injunctions is the following: "All *these abominations* have the men of the land done, which were before you, and the land is defiled. . . . For whosoever shall commit any of *these abominations*, even the souls that commit them shall be cut off from among their people. Therefore shall ye keep mine ordinance, that ye commit not any one of *these abominable customs*, which were committed before you, and that ye defile not yourselves therein: I am the Lord your God." Leviticus 18:27-30. Emphasis supplied. God has one word that He constantly uses for all forms of transgression of the seventh commandment: to Him it is *abomination*.

Sexual Perversion

The total testimony of Scripture reveals that the principle of sexual purity ennunciated in the seventh commandment extends beyond the matter of mere marital infidelity and condemns all forms of sexual perversion. Consider the following partial scriptural evidence:

1. Romans 1:18, 26, 27, 32—Sodomy and lesbianism are condemned.
2. Leviticus 18:22-26, 29; 20:13, 14, 23-26—Homosexuality is an abomination to God.
3. 1 Corinthians 6:9, 10—"Abusers" shall not enter the kingdom of God. Compare Revelation 22:14, 15.
4. Genesis 19:1-29—Sexual perversion was among the sins which resulted in the destruction of Sodom and Gomorrah. Compare Jude 7.
5. Leviticus 18:24-28—Sexual perversion was among the sins for which God destroyed the nations of Canaan.

The question might well be raised as to why, if all forms of sexual perversion are so displeasing to God, He limited the seventh commandment to adultery and did not include these other deviations in the divine prohibition. The answer is to be found in the fact that the sexual relationship between a man and a woman is normal and natural. When God forbids the illicit misuse of that which is normal and natural, He is automatically embracing in that prohibition anything else that is abnormal and unnatural. He is saying in effect, If the misuse of that which is normal and natural is sin, *how much more* sinful is the abnormal and unnatual perversion of that gift.

Does the Bible Condone Polygamy?

Doesn't the fact that God didn't condemn men in Old Testament times who had more than one wife, and don't passages of Scripture such as 1 Timothy 3:2, which seems to restrict monogamy to bishops, indicate that polygamy is acceptable to God?

The total testimony of Scripture is to the effect that God's purpose was a monogamous union between a man and woman for life and that the departure from this plan was one of the baleful and bitter results of the entrance of sin. When the Christian church was established, God designed that His original plan would be exalted and restored. In his statement in 1 Timothy 3:2, Paul is not condoning polygamy by the rank and file of church membership. Rather, he is insisting that leaders set the right example to the church in the pattern of their homelife. All New Testament references to the husband-and-wife relationship always and only refer to the husband and the wife in the *singular* form. See 1 Corinthians 7:14; Ephesians 5:23; 1 Timothy 5:9; Titus 1:6; 1 Peter 3:7; Revelation 21:9.

The picture that emerges in bold relief from the Creation record in Genesis 2, endorsed by Jesus in Mark 10, and supported by the New Testament writers, is that God made one man and one woman to be partners for life. This was the module on which all future reproductions of the original was to be based. Any departure from this plan came about as a result of the intrusion of sin and falls short of the Maker's design.

Paul's Attitude to Marriage

It might be felt by some that Paul is deprecating marriage in 1 Corinthians 7. We must, however, balance his apparently antimarital statements in this chapter with his very clear and forthright statement in 1 Timothy 4:1-3, where he *condemns* "forbidding to marry" as one for the "doctrines of devils." If Paul were promoting celibacy in 1 Corinthians 7, he would fall under the condemnation of his own statement in 1 Timothy 4. We must therefore be careful not to read into his admonition to the Corinthian church more than is there. He simply wants his readers to know that it is possible for people to live rich, happy, fruitful lives even though they may, because of circumstances or from personal choice, walk the pilgrim road alone. Marriage isn't necessarily "the be all and end all" of existence. It is possible to be happy and to serve the Lord effectively as a single person. Having made this point, he proceeds to outline the normality of sexual experience in marriage as being perfectly in harmony with Christian experience.

The Inner Self

The life-style that harmonizes with the witness of God's Word hallows and enriches all of life's relationships. It ensures enjoyment of the genuine and protects against the counterfeit enjoyment of the spurious. Only the right to love makes it right to love. Only what we have the right to enjoy gives lasting enjoyment. Forbidden pleasures can give only momentary enjoyment.

We are not mere animals. We are creatures with an inner self. Because this is so, illicit pleasure always has a backlash. It sets off within us reactions that inevitably destroy our happiness, our peace, and our inner strength. The thing that makes this situation even more complex is that these reactions do not usually reveal themselves on the surface of our lives, but in the deep recesses of our inner selves. This explains many of the neuroses, psychoses, and emotional and mental disturbances that we see all around us. If everybody walked in the way of God's commandments there would be little need of psychiatrists and psychiatric clinics. "Great peace have those who love thy law; nothing can make them stumble." Psalm 119:165, RSV. "O that thou hadst hearkened to my commandments! then had thy peace been as a river." Isaiah 48:18.

Walking in the way of God's commandments safeguards not only the home and the spiritual health of the individual, but also the priceless treasure of human friendship. The gift of friendship, both between persons of the same and of the opposite sex, is one of the most precious things the human heart is capable of enjoying. When the protective walls of God's law are set aside, the tides of passion are allowed to sweep in and carry this treasure away, leaving only the silt of regret and self-condemnation. When it is built on the foundation of harmony with God's will, it stands aloof from that which is sensuous and carnal. It dwells on a higher plane, the Bethany plane—that of the friendship between Jesus and His friends Lazarus, Mary, and Martha.

The record says, "Jesus loved Martha, and her sister, and Lazarus." John 11:5. This was a pure, untainted love. "His heart was knit by a strong bond of affection to the family at Bethany. . . . At the home of Lazarus, Jesus had often found rest. . . . Often, when weary, thirsting for human fellowship, He had been glad to escape to this peaceful household, away from the suspicion and jealousy of the angry Pharisees. Here He found a sincere welcome, and pure, holy friendship. Here He could speak with simplicity and perfect freedom, knowing that His words would be understood and treasured.

"Our Saviour appreciated a quiet home and interested listeners. He longed for human tenderness, courtesy, and affection.

. . . In the home at Bethany Christ found rest from the weary conflict of public life."—*The Desire of Ages*, pp. 524, 525.

Such friendship is too sacred to mar. Don't spoil it by soiling it!

Purity of heart and life is a priority to the disciple of Jesus. The Bible doesn't mumble and mutter in the call it makes to followers of the Master to be pure in thought, word, and deed. To the psalmist's question, "Who shall ascend into the hill of the Lord? or who shall stand in his holy place?" the answer comes back loud and clear, "he that hath clean hands, and a pure heart. . . . He shall receive the blessing from the Lord, and righteousness from the God of his salvation." Psalm 24:3-5.

David himself pleaded with God, "Purge me with hyssop, and I shall be clean: wash me, and I shall be whiter than snow." Psalm 51:7. Through the prophet Malachi the Lord declares that "he shall sit as a refiner and purifier of silver: and he shall purify the sons of Levi, and purge them as gold and silver, that they may offer unto the Lord an offering in righteousness." Malachi 3:3. Paul's call to Timothy was to be an example in purity (1 Timothy 4:12) and "keep thyself pure" (1 Timothy 5:22).

The same writer tells us that Jesus "gave himself for us, that he might redeem us from all iniquity, and purify unto himself a peculiar people, zealous of good works." Titus 2:14. With equal emphasis John declares that "every man that hath this hope in him [that of seeing Jesus] purifieth himself, even as he is pure." 1 John 3:3. And Jesus Himself leaves us in no doubt that it is the pure in heart who will see God. See Matthew 5:8.

"This commandment [the seventh] forbids not only acts of impurity, but sensual thoughts and desires, or any practice that tends to excite them. Purity is demanded not only in the outward life but in the secret intents and emotions of the heart. Christ, who taught the far-reaching obligation of the law of God, declared the evil thought or look to be as truly sin as is the unlawful deed."—*Patriarchs and Prophets*, p. 308.

"When the thought of evil is loved and cherished, however secretly, said Jesus, it shows that sin still reigns in the heart. The soul is still in the gall of bitterness and in the bond of iniquity. He who finds pleasure in dwelling upon scenes of impurity, who indulges the evil thought, the lustful look, may behold in the open sin, with its burden of shame and heart-breaking grief, the true nature of the evil which he has hidden in the chambers of the soul. The season of temptation, under which, it may be, one falls into grievous sin, does not create the evil that is revealed, but only develops or makes manifest that which was hidden and latent in the heart. As a man 'thinketh in his heart, so is he;' for out of the heart 'are the issues of life.' Proverbs 23:7; 4:23."—*Thoughts From the Mount of Blessing*, p. 60.

It is when sinful thoughts are cherished, meditated upon, that they constitute sin. We cannot keep the birds from flying over our heads, but we can prevent them from nesting in our hair. Any thought meditated upon will in time produce a deed. If the deed it would produce is a sinful deed, the thought pattern that would produce it is a sinful thought pattern. Daily we should pray, "Let the words of my mouth, and the meditation of my heart, be acceptable in thy sight, O Lord, my strength, and my redeemer." Psalm 19:14.

The moral climate in which we live is not one that encourages or stimulates purity. On the contrary, it fosters the very opposite. Impurity is glamorized on the TV screen and the radio and by what is sold on the literature racks. Yet God's people need not become polluted by the sin that surrounds them. We need not become acclimatized to the spirit of our corrupt age. By hiding God's word in our hearts we may be kept from sinning against Him. See Psalm 119:11. The story of Joseph beautifully illustrates this truth. See Genesis 39:7-9.

Two things enabled Joseph to come through this encounter with temptation unscathed. First, he recognized sin as sin. He did not have a hazy notion as to what was right and wrong. Sin was clearly defined in his thinking. He did not meet sin apologetically or tongue in cheek. He called sin by its right name. Second, he was living to please God, not himself. He made it clear that any deviation from principle would be displeasing to God. This is what mattered. He had his priorities straight.

Modern youth may feel that they are subjected to much greater stresses today than were the young people who lived in Bible times. It must be borne in mind, though, that for Joseph there was no reason for doing right and shunning wrong apart from his love for God. He could have rationalized that as a slave he had few enjoyments. From the purely human point of view there was nothing for him to lose. His brothers had sold him as a slave. He would probably never see his father again. The opportunity to enjoy himself with a lovely Egyptian woman must have been exceedingly flattering to his wounded ego.

Nothing but a deep love for God would keep a young man unsullied in the face of such overwhelming odds. Nothing less is needed today.

The counsels given by the apostle Paul in the texts below all contain one word which would be a good watchword for young disciples today. That word aptly describes the action Joseph took when tempted. That word is flee. See 1 Corinthians 6:18-20; 1 Timothy 6:11, 12; 2 Timothy 2:22. The verbs used in Scripture to describe the Christian's attitude toward sin and righteousness are powerful, active verbs, such as those in these texts. Notice them: Flee, Follow, Fight, Lay Hold. There is nothing in these texts that suggests we are just to stand around waiting for God to perform a miracle to save us from falling into sin. The responsibility is placed on us to do our part by fleeing from sin when it comes our way. See Romans 13:14.

The challenge that confronts the church in the field of human sexuality involves all aspects of social relationships between men and women in the community and in the church. One general principle can be laid down which covers them all: God demands the strictest purity in His people.

God expects His people to mold their moral conduct and their interpersonal relationships by the standards of His Word and not by the eroding sense of values everywhere apparent in the society in which we live.

"Don't let the world around you squeeze you into its own mold, but let God remold your minds from within, so that you may prove in practice that the plan of God for you is good, meets all his demands and moves toward the goal of true maturity." Romans 12:2, Phillips.

This Scripture teaches that God has called us to holiness. In no field of human experience do we have a greater or fuller opportunity to demonstrate our response to His calling than in that which involves our relationship with and our attitudes toward those among whom we live—in our homes, in our church, and in our community.

If You Have Transgressed

If, as you have read this chapter, your heart has been filled with guilt and shame, don't despair. Do you stand before God condemned as a transgresor of the seventh commandment? God cannot countenance your sin, but He has not forsaken you. There is pardon for all who seek His forgiveness in sincere and humble repentance. Here is His promise: "Let the wicked forsake his way, and the unrighteous man his thoughts: and let him return unto the Lord, and he will have mercy upon him; and to our God, for he will abundantly pardon." Isaiah 55:7.

Notice how simple are the conditions of forgiveness. God doesn't ask you to afflict your soul. He doesn't ask you to publish your sins in the press. He doesn't ask you to confess your sins to any mortal, not even to your minister. He asks you to (1) *forsake* your sin and (2) *return* to the Lord. That is all. These are God's terms. Now notice God's provisions: He will have mercy, and He will *abundantly* pardon. No one need despair. In Christ there is pardon, peace, and power; cleansing, freedom, and victory.

After King David had brought reproach on the name of God by breaking the seventh commandment, he said, "I acknowledged my sin unto thee, and mine iniquity have I not hid. I said, I will confess my transgressions unto the Lord; and thou forgavest the iniquity of my sin." "Blessed is he whose transgression is forgiven, whose sin is covered." Psalm 32:5, 1. You, too, can know the blessedness of the forgiveness that comes from forsaking sin and turning to the Lord. To find God, take the first turn to the "right" and keep moving forward, "forgetting those things which are behind."

In two direct encounters with transgressors of the seventh commandment, Jesus demonstrated His tender loving concern for the guilty and His willingness to forgive. You can read these two beautiful stories in John 8:3-11 and John 4:5-42.

"This was to her [the woman taken in adultery] the beginning of a new life, a life of purity and peace, devoted to the service of

God. In the uplifting of this fallen soul, Jesus performed a greater miracle than in healing the most grievous physical disease; He cured the spiritual malady which is unto death everlasting. This penitent woman became one of His most steadfast followers. With self-sacrificing love and devotion she repaid His forgiving mercy.

"In His act of pardoning this woman and encouraging her to live a better life, the character of Jesus shines forth in the beauty of perfect righteousness. While He does not palliate sin, nor lessen the sense of guilt, He seeks not to condemn, but to save. The world had for this erring woman only contempt and scorn; but Jesus speaks words of comfort and hope. The Sinless One pities the weakness of the sinner, and reaches to her a helping hand. While the hypocritical Pharisees denounce, Jesus bids her, 'Go, and sin no more.'

"It is not Christ's follower that, with averted eyes, turns from the erring, leaving them unhindered to pursue their downward course. Those who are forward in accusing others, and zealous in bringing them to justice, are often in their own lives more guilty than they. Men hate the sinner, while they love the sin. Christ hates the sin, but loves the sinner. This will be the spirit of all who follow Him. Christian love is slow to censure, quick to discern penitence, ready to forgive, to encourage, to set the wanderer in the path of holiness, and to stay his feet therein."—*The Desire of Ages*, p. 462.

Disappointed in Marriage

"Now, as in Christ's day, the condition of society presents a sad comment upon heaven's ideal of this sacred relation. Yet even for those who have found bitterness and disappointment where they had hoped for companionship and joy, the gospel of Christ offers a solace. The patience and gentleness which His Spirit can impart will sweeten the bitter lot. The heart in which Christ dwells will be so filled, so satisfied with His love that it will not be consumed with longing to attract sympathy and attention to itself. And through the surrender of the soul to God, His wisdom can accomplish what human wisdom fails to do. Through the revelation of His grace, hearts that were once indifferent or estranged may be united in bonds that are firmer and more enduring than those of earth—the golden bonds of a love that will bear the test of trial."—*Thoughts From the Mount of Blessing*, p. 65.

Whether happily or unhappily married, whether living with a marriage partner or alone, the one privilege we can all enjoy and which we must not forfeit at any cost is fellowship with Christ. The rewards of walking in the paths of purity are abundant, both in this life and in the life to come. Don't allow yourself to be cheated out of them!

Chapter X

Walking with Jesus is not a cloud-nine experience. The religion of Jesus is not divorced from reality. It enables the disciple of the Master to be a man among men. It enters into every sphere and relationship of the believer's life. This includes his professional, business, and vocational life. A Christian should be the most honest man in his community. Like David Hewitt, the first Sabbath keeper in Battle Creek, Michigan, every Seventh-day Adventist Christian should be known in his community as the most honest man in town!

Shady deals and unlawful profit are outside his terms of reference. Words such as *cheating, bribery* and *corruption* do not exist in his vocabulary. His business transactions are open at all times to the scrutiny of the One who walks at his side. "Let us walk honestly, as in the day," is the standard that is set for us in Romans 13:13.

Of Enoch the record says that he "walked with God" (Genesis 5:24) and that he "pleased God" (Hebrews 11:5). Yet Enoch's walk with God was not a divorced-from-reality experience. It was a relationship with God that influenced his relationship with men. His life was transparent.

"Enoch's walk with God was not in a trance or a vision, but in all the duties of his daily life. He did not become a hermit, shutting himself entirely from the world; for he had a work to do for God in the world. . . . As a husband and father, a friend, a citizen, he was the steadfast, unwavering servant of the Lord.

"In the midst of a life of active labor, Enoch steadfastly maintained his communion with God. The greater and more pressing his labors, the more constant and earnest were his prayers."—*Patriarchs and Prophets*, pp. 85, 86.

The call to walk honestly (Romans 13:13) has a special eschatological setting. It is given in the context of the last day. "The night is far spent, the day is at hand: let us therefore cast off the works of darkness, and let us put on the armour of light." Verse 12.

"The godly character of this prophet [Enoch] represents the state of holiness which must be attained by those who shall be 'redeemed from the earth' (Revelation 14:3) at the time of Christ's second advent. . . . Like Enoch, God's people will seek for purity of heart and conformity to His will, until they shall reflect the likeness of Christ."—*Patriarchs and Prophets*, pp. 88, 89.

The matter of "conformity to His will" and of reflecting "the likeness of Christ," involves the eighth commandment, which says, "Thou shalt not steal." Exodus 20:15.

The New Testament stresses the obligation that rests on disciples to have a reputation for honesty! Notice these verses:

"Having your conversation [life-style] honest among the Gentiles [unbelievers]: that . . . they may by your good works, which they shall behold, glorify God." 1 Peter 2:12.

"Providing for honest things, not only in the sight of the Lord, but also in the sight of men." 2 Corinthians 8:21. See also 2 Corinthians 13:7; Romans 12:17; 1 Thessalonians 4:12; 1 Timothy 2:2; Hebrews 13:18. The same principle is repeated in all these passages of Scripture! The frequency with which honesty is mentioned by Bible writers tells us something about the importance God attaches to this virtue in the life of one who professes to be His follower. God realized how easily the dishonesty of the world around us could rub off onto even a devout disciple of the Master unless he was constantly on his guard against it!

More ingredients than "not stealing" enter into what constitutes genuine honesty!

"That ye may walk honestly toward them that are without, and that ye may have lack of nothing." "And that ye study to be quiet, and to do your own business, and to work with your own hands, as we commanded you." 1 Thessalonians 4:12, 11.

Five things are here included in what "we command you." They are not merely injunctions but *commands*:

1. *We command you* "that ye walk honestly toward them that are without." As Christians be honest in your dealings with non-Christians.

2. *We command you* to strive to "have lack of nothing." Aim, as far as is humanly possible, to be independent and to stand on your own two feet, so that you won't need to beg from or lean on others for support.

3. *We command you* to "study to be quiet." Don't be a busybody or a mischief-maker.

4. *We command you* "to do your own business," or, as we would say today, "mind your own business!"

5. *We command you* "to work with your own hands." Honest toil is one of God's imperatives that is enjoined on every believer. The Bible teaches the dignity of labor. Christianity, properly understood, is not a religion that produces lazy men! Diligence is often enjoined in the Word of God as an essential ingredient of honesty. For further examples see 2 Corinthians 8:22 and Proverbs 22:29.

Jesus also had much to tell us about our duty to be honest in discharging our responsibilities as citizens of our country! See Matthew 22:21; Mark 12:17; Luke 20:25; Matthew 17:24-27.

Does a Christian have the right to withhold the payment of his taxes because he does not agree with the system of government practiced by his country?

The Bible says much concerning the matter of God's people dealing fairly with those who work for them. Dire judgment is pronounced against employers who withhold their rightful wage from those who have earned it. "Go to now, ye rich men, weep and howl for your miseries that shall come upon you. Your riches are corrupted, and your garments are motheaten. Your gold and silver is cankered; and the rust of them shall be a witness against you, and shall eat your flesh as it were fire. Ye have heaped treasure together for the last days. Behold, the hire of the labourers who have reaped down your fields, which is of you kept back by fraud, crieth: and the cries of them which have reaped are entered into the ears of the Lord of sabaoth." James 5:1-4.

God's Word does not condemn anyone for being rich. It teaches that riches are often the result of God's blessing. See Proverbs 10:22; Psalm 1:1-3. It only condemns becoming rich by dishonest means. God hates any act which benefits one person at the cost of taking advantage of someone else. "A false balance is abomination to the Lord: but a just weight is his delight." Proverbs 11:1.

Employer and Employee

In the New Testament, earnest appeals to fair play are directed to Christians who have other people working under them. "Ye masters, do the same things unto them, forbearing threatening: knowing that your Master also is in heaven; neither is there respect of persons with him." Ephesians 6:9.

In the Old Testament, God insisted on strict honesty and justice among the Israelites in all their dealing with their fellowmen. "Thou shalt not defraud thy neighbour, neither rob him: the wages of him that is hired shall not abide with thee all night until the morning." Leviticus 19:13.

It is possible for an employee, on the other hand, while deploring the fact that his employer defrauds him in the matter of wages, to defraud his employer in the matter of time and productivity! Shortchanging in time is just as much dishonesty as shortchanging in money!

"We are under the most solemn obligation to improve it [our time] to His [God's] glory. Of no talent He has given will He require a more strict account than of our time.

"The value of time is beyond computation. Christ regarded every moment as precious, and it is thus that we should regard it. Life is too short to be trifled away. . . .

"It is the duty of every Christian to acquire habits of order, thoroughness, and dispatch. There is no excuse for slow bungling at work of any character."—*Christ's Object Lessons*, pp. 342-344.

The Vertical Dimension

The principle of honesty has a vertical as well as a horizontal dimension. It enters into my relationship with God as well as with my fellowmen.

"Will a man rob God? Yet ye have robbed me. But ye say, Wherein have we robbed thee? In tithes and offerings." "Bring ye all the tithes into the storehouse, that there may be meat in mine house, and prove me now herewith, saith the Lord of hosts, if I will not open you the windows of heaven, and pour you out a blessing, that there shall not be room enough to receive it." Malachi 3:8, 10.

We are not being generous when we return a tithe to God; we are merely being honest. Generosity begins only after we have returned to God what He rightfully claims as His!

A pastor received a phone call from a very wealthy church member who asked him to come over and see him urgently. When the minister was seated in the businessman's teak-paneled, plush-carpeted study, the troubled brother opened his heart to his pastor and told him he had a serious problem. He said when he got his first job in his youth, he promised the Lord a tithe of all he ever earned. From his first pay of five dollars, he duly gave God fifty cents. He had been richly blessed, and through the years his earnings had increased until now he was paying tithe of $500,000 a year! "Pastor," he said, "I just can't afford to continue giving away all that money! Is there some way I could rescind my pledge?" The pastor was thoughtful for a moment and then he answered, "No, brother, there's no way you could revoke your pledge. But I'll tell you what we could do. We could go down on our knees and ask the Lord to once again reduce your earnings to only five dollars so as to make it easier for you to pay your tithe!"

We can't play games with God!

The way in which we disburse our tithe is not left to our discretion. See Leviticus 27:30; Numbers 18:21; 1 Corinthians 9:11-14; Malachi 3:10. From these passages of Scripture it is clear that it is not our prerogative to put one tenth of our income into a "charity box" at home and disburse it to various "worthy causes" as opportunity arises. God claims the first tenth of all our income as belonging to Him. He doesn't give us the right to pay all our bills first and then give Him a tithe out of what is left.

He also reserves the right to specify how it shall be allocated. Regarding the use to which it is to be put, He has left us in no doubt whatever. It is specifically designated as being for the support of His church, for the proclamation of the gospel, and for the sustenance of those who proclaim it. What we give to charity and to community projects is over and above the tithe which the Lord claims as His.

Honest From Within

Honesty, like all other virtues, is not something we put on like a cloak. It's not something we practice because it is the best policy. It is not merely one of the rules of the game, which we play so as not to be penalized. It must come from the heart. It is a principle of life, of being. "Finally, brethren," admonishes Paul, "whatsoever things are true, whatsoever things are honest, whatsoever things are just, whatsoever things are pure, whatsoever things are lovely, whatsoever things are of good report; if there be any virtue, and if there be any praise, think on these things." Philippians 4:8.

If we think honest thoughts, we will perform honest acts. If any temptation to perform a dishonest deed is repulsed with the first insinuation of the thought and if we cultivate the frame of mind of thinking on "whatsoever things are honest," we will be honest in our dealings. As stated earlier, keeping the Ten Commandments is not so much a matter of doing as of being. And it is by walking with Jesus that we become what He is. By being with Him, we become like Him and come to reflect the attributes of His own character in our lives.

This gives to life a dimension none but those who walk with Jesus on the path of obedience can know. It is the only life of genuine enjoyment and fulfillment.

Chapter XI

Solomon declares that there are seven things the Lord hates and which are "an abomination" to Him: (1) a proud look, (2) a lying tongue, (3) hands that shed innocent blood, (4) a heart that devises wicked imaginations, (5) feet that are swift in running to mischief, (6) a false witness that speaks lies, (7) sowing discord among brethren. Proverbs 6:16-19. Elsewhere Solomon states that "lying lips are abomination to the Lord." Proverbs 12:22.

It is noteworthy that of these seven, four relate directly to the spoken word and to the ninth commandment, which forbids the bearing of false witness. Mischiefmaking and sowing discord among brethren are just as displeasing to God as the more flagrant sin of falsifying judicial evidence.

The ninth commandment condemns not only deliberate misrepresentation but also the repetition of unverified information which would harm a person. The precept "Thou shalt not bear false witness" is concerned with more than just the bearing of witness in court. Certainly the giving of false evidence in court is wrong in the sight of God, and He will not let it go unpunished, unless repented of, confessed, and forsaken. Especially is this true when false evidence is presented wilfully and under solemn oath. God's Word teaches that liars will have their part in "the lake of fire." See Revelation 21:8, 27. This applies to both those who lie inside and outside of court.

Not only does God hate direct, overt lying. He equally hates the relaying of information which has not been established as fact and is designed to harm a person. We call it gossip. Long ago when

God separated Israel to be His special people, He stressed His abhorence of this evil among His people: "Thou shalt not raise a false report: put not thine hand with the wicked to be an unrighteous witness." Exodus 23:1. "Thou shalt not go up and down as a talebearer among thy people: neither shalt thou stand against the blood of thy neighbour: I am the Lord." Leviticus 19:16.

How pertinent is the warning of the New Testament writer James! "The tongue is a little member, and boasteth great things. Behold, how great a matter a little fire kindleth! And the tongue is a fire, a world of iniquity: so is the tongue among our members, that it defileth the whole body, and setteth on fire the course of nature; and it is set on fire of hell. For every kind of beasts, and of birds, and of serpents, and of things in the sea, is tamed, and hath been tamed by mankind: but the tongue can no man tame; it is an unruly evil, full of deadly poison. Therewith bless we God, even the Father; and therewith curse we men, which are made after the similitude of God. Out of the same mouth proceedeth blessing and cursing. My brethren, these things ought not so to be." James 3:5-10.

In the sight of God evil surmising is as evil as the evil we surmise. Suggestion, insinuation, innuendo, and inference may constitute as real a transgression of the ninth commandment as downright lying.

We never have the right to repeat hearsay until it has been established as fact beyond any shadow of a doubt. How many hearts and homes have been broken up, how many reputations ruined, what a harvest of discord and unhappiness has been sown by the ravaging evil of gossip. How easy it is to base our conclusions on observation and come to the wrong conclusion! Before we open our mouths to repeat anything we should always ask ourselves three questions: Is it true? Is it kind? Is it necessary? When we have prayerfully considered these questions, we may proceed to speak—if we still desire to do so! Well may we pray the prayer of the psalmist: "Set a watch, O Lord, before my mouth; keep the door of my lips." Psalm 141:3. "Let the words of my mouth, and the meditation of my heart, be acceptable in thy sight, O Lord, my strength, and my redeemer." Psalm 19:14.

Another aspect of the subject bears consideration. "There shall in no wise enter into it [the Holy City] any thing that defileth . . . or *maketh* a lie." Revelation 21:27. Emphasis supplied. It is possible to tell lies, and it is possible to make lies. In the first instance the untruth is by word, in the second by life. We call it deception. It involves giving the wrong impression, even though the words may be truthful enough. We fall under this condemnation when we pretend to be what we are not, when we profess to be Christians and yet cherish in our lives those things which we know are contrary to God's revealed will.

Let us ever be sure that not only our words, but also our acts tell the truth. If I disconnect the speedometer of my automobile so that when I sell it, it registers 10,000 miles less than it has actually run, is not that as much bearing false witness as if I lied with my lips? Is it really worth getting an extra $100 for my car and losing my place in the city into which not "any thing that defileth . . . nor maketh a lie" will ever enter? What a price to pay!

Jesus makes it clear that those who engage in any form of untruthfulness are pursuing a course blazed by Satan, the original liar. Said Jesus, speaking to those who deviated from the pathway of truth: "Ye are of your father the devil, and the lusts of your father ye will do. He was a murderer from the beginning, and abode not in the truth, because there is no truth in him. When he speaketh a lie, he speaketh of his own: for he is a liar, and the father of it." John 8:44.

In glowing contrast with this description of Satan as "the father of lies," Jesus is described as "the truth." John 14:6. It is our privilege to be followers of Him who is the very personification of truth, rather than of him who is the parent of untruth!

Not only does the Bible condemn those who bear false witness of any kind, but it commends those who refrain from sinning with their lips against their neighbor: "Lord, who shall abide in thy tabernacle? who shall dwell in thy holy hill? He that walketh uprightly, and worketh righteousness, and speaketh the truth in his heart. He that backbiteth not with his tongue, nor doeth evil to his neighbour, nor taketh up a reproach against his neighbour. . . . He that doeth these things shall never be moved." Psalm 15:1-5.

The Bible gives us golden counsel on the matter of repeating information of which we become aware: "He that covereth a transgression seeketh love; but he that repeateth a matter separateth very friends." Proverbs 17:9.

Imagine how much heartache would be spared if this counsel were taken seriously—and were strictly carried out!

The notion that is applied by many is that when we "know something about someone" it is our duty to tell! Thus it is generally accepted by those who follow this principle that, if a student knows that another has cheated in an examination, it is his duty to tell the teacher; if a workman knows that his workmate has stolen, it is his duty to tell the boss, and so on. But, strange as it may sound, this is not the principle which is to govern the life of a Christian! Notice the principle outlined by our leader Jesus Christ in Matthew 18:15 and by the apostle Paul in Galatians 6:1, 2.

According to the principle they lay down, the first person to whom we should speak when we know he has done wrong, is the person himself, and *he* should be given the opportunity to make the wrong right himself! If the person with whom we dicuss his wrong course of action in a spirit of loving concern displays a spirit of genuine repentance, we have achieved our purpose and *should say not another word about the matter to anyone*. If the wrongdoer persists in his evil course, Jesus says that we should take a witness with us. Maybe he will listen to two people where he wouldn't give heed to one. Only when this has been done, and he still refuses to heed the counsel given, should we take the matter further. How much irreparable harm would have been avoided in homes, communities, and churches if this divine blueprint had always been faithfully followed!

Notice how James sums up the results of pursuing this heaven-ordained course of action: "Brethren, if any of you do err from the truth, and one convert him; let him know, that he which converteth the sinner from the error of his way, shall save a soul from death, and shall hide a multitude of sins." James 5:19, 20.

The Word of God holds out a high ideal to the Christian!

"But speaking the truth in love, may grow up into him in all things, which is the head, even Christ." "Wherefore putting away lying, speak every man truth with his neighbour: for we are members one of another." "Let no corrupt communication proceed out of your mouth, but that which is good to the use of edifying, that it may minister grace unto the hearer." Ephesians 4:15, 25, 29.

It can be the happy privilege of every disciple of the Master, high and low, to reach out to the attainment of that heaven-ordained ideal!

"Life's best things—simplicity, honesty, truthfulness, purity, integrity—cannot be bought or sold. They are as free to the ignorant as to the educated, to the humble laborer as to the honored statesman."—*The Ministry of Healing*, p. 198.

His Master's Voice

The disciple of Jesus is not only under obligation to refrain from speaking evil, but has laid upon him the joyous assignment of being his Master's voice to utter the words Jesus would speak in his situation! What a high and holy privilege! "Let your speech be alway with grace," says the apostle Paul, "seasoned with salt." Colossians 4:6.

The Bible uses beautiful imagery to portray the influence for good our words may be! Observe:

"A word fitly spoken is like apples of gold in pictures of silver." Proverbs 25:11.

"The words of a man's mouth are as deep waters, and the wellspring of wisdom as a flowing brook." Proverbs 18:4.

"The words of the pure are pleasant words." Proverbs 15:26.

"Heaviness in the heart of man maketh it stoop: but a good word maketh it glad." Proverbs 12:25.

To make texts like these come true must surely be one of life's greatest delights! Imagine being able to have a part in expressing the love of Christ for lost humanity! What could possibly be more like heaven on earth than that!

Chapter XII

Let us allow our imagination to run away with us for a few minutes to a wonderful world that might have been and that could still be, if only . . .

Try to imagine what the world would be like if everybody kept the Ten Commandments!

—No war, no riots, no crime, no murder, no hatred . . .

—No burglary, no stealing, no dishonesty, no shortchanging, no cheating, no shady deals . . .

—No adultery, no fornication, no sexual perversion, no rape, no criminal assault, no abortion, no illegitimacy, no veneral diseases, no infidelity, no broken promises, no broken hearts, no broken homes, no broken lives, no disillusioned hopes . . .

—No envy, no jealousy, no covetousness, no avarice, no greed, no selfishness . . .

—No idolatry, no blasphemy, no atheism, no agnosticism, no disloyalty, no disobedience, no anarchy, no rebellion, no disharmony, no ruptured relationships, no SIN!

Almost too good to be true! Yet all it would take to make it a reality would be for each reader of these lines to keep the Ten Commandments, and then persuade only two other people to follow his example; for each of those two to persuade two others in turn; each of those, two others, and each of those two others, and for this process to be repeated for a total of only twenty-one times! By then every man, woman, and child of earth's over four and a half billion people would be keeping God's law, and we would have the kind of world we all wish we could live in! Now you know why I spoke about our imagination running away with us! But why can't it be that way? Will it ever happen? Let's look at these two questions for a moment.

What prevents such a marvelous thing from happening? The tenth commandment provides the answer! This final commandment takes us to the heart of things. It is not by accident that God placed the precept "Thou shalt not covet" at the end of His law. Not only does it summarize everything that has gone before, but it focuses attention on the spot where all obedience (and all disobedience) begins and *ends*—the human heart. It takes us to the roots. The New Testament writer James makes this clear when he writes this in chapter 4 of his epistle:

"From whence come wars and fightings among you? come they not hence, even of your lusts that war in your members? Ye lust, and have not: ye kill, and desire to have, and cannot obtain: ye fight and war, yet ye have not, because ye ask not. Ye ask, and receive not, because ye ask amiss, that ye may consume it upon your lusts. Ye adulterers and adulteresses, know ye not that the friendship of the world is enmity with God? whosoever therefore will be a friend of the world is the enemy of God. Do ye think that the scripture saith in vain, The spirit that dwelleth in us lusteth to envy?" Verses 1-5.

Notice that "wars and fightings" (the transgression of the sixth commandment), and adultery (the transgression of the seventh), have their source in "the spirit that dwelleth in us" which "lusteth to envy." Here is the crux of our whole problem, the nucleus of all our trouble. Here is the cancer that is poisoning our entire earthly system—personal, social, national, and international.

Jesus identifies the heart as the brood chamber of sin. See Matthew 5:28; 12:34, 35. The apostle Paul associates himself with James and Jesus when he says this: "What shall we say then? Is the law sin? God forbid. Nay, I had not known sin, but by the law: for I had not known lust, except the law had said, Thou shalt not covet." Romans 7:7.

"The tenth commandment strikes at the very root of all sins, prohibiting the selfish desire, from which springs the sinful act. He who in obedience to God's law refrains from indulging even a sinful desire for that which belongs to another will not be guilty of an act of wrong toward his fellow creatures."—*Patriarchs and Prophets*, p. 309.

Sometimes we hear people say that the Ten Commandments cannot be kept. It is impossible, they declare, and therefore God does not require obedience from us! But let us ask a question: When we say that the law cannot be kept, is it because there is something wrong with the law, or because there is something wrong with us? Must the law be abolished to accomodate us, or must we be changed to measure up with God's requirements? Must the law be brought down to our low level, or is it we who need to be brought up to the high and holy standard of God's law? Must God bend His straight rule to our crooked will, or must He bend our crooked will to comply with His straight rule? Must the darkness be allowed to swallow up the light, or must the light be made to shatter the darkness?

The tenth commandment exposes the roots of religion and irreligion. It reveals that the kernel of all sin is selfishness. "All selfishness is covetousness, and is, therefore, idolatry."—*Counsels on Stewardship*, p. 223. "Self-idolatry . . . lies at the foundation of all sin."—*Testimonies*, vol. 9, p. 27.

What we really mean when we say we "cannot keep the Ten Commandments" is that our selfish hearts need to be surrendered for crucifixion. Self must die. Self-love, self-seeking, self-pity, self-exaltation, and all other species of self-worship must be crucified with Christ. It is here at the tenth commandment that the law is linked to the cross. Here Sinai and Calvary meet.

The tenth commandment opens to our view the great controversy between Christ and Satan. The battlefield is the human heart. Here is settled the question of our allegiance. Whom we choose as sovereign of our hearts decides the question of whether we are going to obey God, which means renouncing Satan; or obey Satan, which means renouncing God. "Know ye not, that to whom ye yield yourselves servants to obey, his servants ye are to whom ye obey; whether of sin unto death, or of obedience unto righteousness?" Romans 6:16.

So, the matter of keeping the Ten Commandments, or not keeping them, is a matter of settling the question of our allegiance. It centers around the question of to whom we yield ourselves. This is where so many earnest people fail. They think that keeping the commandments is a matter of putting forward a desperate effort. Such human efforts can produce only abject failure and disillusionment at worst, and hollow, lifeless legalism at best. What we need to do in order to keep the Ten Commandments is not struggle but surrender! When this has happened, we will say this along with Paul the apostle: "For I through the law am dead to the law, that I might live unto God. I am crucified with Christ: nevertheless I live; yet not I, but Christ liveth in me: and the life which I now live in the flesh I live by the faith of the Son of God, who loved me, and gave himself for me. I do not frustrate the grace of God: for if righteousness come by the law, then Christ is dead in vain." Galatians 2:19-21.

Paul is not here abolishing the law as a standard. Concerning that standard he says that it is holy, just, and good—spiritual. Romans 7:12, 14. But he is renouncing the law as a means of salvation, or righteousness. He is saying, in effect, that the way to measure up to the standard is not through vain human effort so to do, but by allowing ourselves to be crucified with Christ. Then Christ, who perfectly fulfilled the law of God by dwelling in our hearts, enables us, through His indwelling presence, perfectly to fulfill the requirements of His law in our lives. This is what God means when He promises to write His law in our hearts. Our souls respond to the sovereign authority of the Conqueror who has become the King of our lives.

When people tell us we cannot keep the Ten Commandments are they right or wrong? Right! Why? Because "the heart is deceitful above all things, and desperately wicked: who can know it?" Jeremiah 17:9. What is the solution? Do away with the law that condemns our hearts to death? No! "Do we make void the law through faith? God forbid: yea, we establish the law." Romans 3:31. What then? Hand over for crucifixion the sinful nature that is condemned to death by the law! "Knowing this, that our old man is crucified with him, that the body of sin might be destroyed, that henceforth we should not serve sin." "For sin shall not have dominion over you: for ye are not under the law, but under grace." Romans 6:6, 14.

There is no need to misunderstand the expression "not under the law, but under grace." Let us follow Paul's reasoning. When sin has "dominion over us" we are under the condemnation of the law. When we refuse to allow sin to have dominion over us, we are no longer under the condemnation of the law, but under the protective covering of grace.

This can be illustrated in a very simple way: When I obey the traffic regulations, I am under the grace, or favor, of the men who administer the rules of the road. They are my friends and my protectors. I may even pause to bid one of them the time of day, and even though he looks very imposing in his uniform, he may exchange a friendly greeting with me. But supposing I transgress the rules of the road by dashing through a red traffic light or by exceeding the speed limit, I immediately fall from grace, and the big hands of the traffic officer become not hands of greeting but of condemnation!

What it all boils down to is this: Whether or not we "are able" to keep the commandments of God is a question of relationship. When self reigns on the throne and Christ stands on the threshold of my life, obedience to God's requirements is an absolute impossibility. I obey not the law of God, but the law of inclination. Whenever I face a choice between right and wrong, it is my feelings, my tastes, my desires that are consulted and obeyed.

But when self is dethroned and relegated to the threshold of my life and Christ is enthroned, what happens? When faced with a choice between right and wrong I no longer consult my desires, but God's will. Before this happened, whenever there was a clash between my desires and God's will, I rejected God's will and yielded to my desires. Now when there is a clash, I reject my desires and accept God's will. With the psalmist I say: "I delight to do thy will, O my God: yea, thy law is within my heart." Psalm 40:8.

This is the only basis of true commandment keeping. No other kind will prepare the soul for eternity. Outward conformity may make a man an honorable citizen of his country here and a church member in good and regular standing. But it is powerless to prepare him for heavenly citizenship. And it is heavenly citizenship that new-covenant Christianity is concerned with.

"However trifling this or that wrong act may seem in the eyes of men, no sin is small in the sight of God. Man's judgment is partial, imperfect; but God estimates all things as they really are. The drunkard is despised and is told that his sin will exclude him from heaven; while pride, selfishness, and covetousness too often go unrebuked. But these are sins that are especially offensive to God; for they are contrary to the benevolence of His character, to that unselfish love which is the very atmosphere of the unfallen universe."—*Steps to Christ*, p. 30.

Away with the notion that new-covenant Christianity abolishes the law! The very converse is true.

"But let none deceive themselves with the thought that God, in His great love and mercy, will yet save even the rejecters of His grace. The exceeding sinfulness of sin can be estimated only in the light of the cross. When men urge that God is too good to cast off the [unrepentant] sinner, let them look to Calvary." "Sin, however small it may be esteemed, can be indulged in only at the peril of infinite loss. What we do not overcome, will overcome us and work out our destruction." "Calvary stands as a memorial of the amazing sacrifice required to atone for the transgression of the divine law. Let us not regard sin as a trivial thing."—*Steps to Christ*, pp. 31, 32, 33.

The Sweet Bye and Bye

Will the time ever come when the idyllic conditions described in our opening paragraph will prevail on earth? God says Yes. "And there shall be no more curse: but the throne of God and of the Lamb shall be in it; and his servants shall serve him." Revelation 22:3. But, alas, it will not be because a process by which each convert has been responsible for the conversion of two other people—and hence the entire race! God would gladly have it that way, but He is not going to claim allegiance of the heart by force. Every man must offer it to God willingly and freely. "Behold, I stand at the door, and knock: if any man hear my voice, and open the door, I will come in to him, and will sup with him, and he with me." Revelation 3:20. Not all will respond to His tender call. Those who don't will eventually be excluded eternally from the bliss and perfection of paradise, which would be marred by their presence there. "For without are dogs, and sorcerers, and whoremongers, and murderers, and idolaters, and whosoever loveth and maketh a lie." Revelation 22:15. "What do ye imagine against the Lord? he will make an utter end: affliction shall not rise up the second time." Nahum 1:9.

Those who inhabit His eternal kingdom there and then will be those who have become prepared for citizenship by obedience to God's will here and now.

The Sweet Here and Now

God hasn't changed His law. He wants to change our hearts. He didn't abolish the royal law of life and liberty by putting Christ on the cross. What He needs to abolish is the law of sin and death in our lives by putting us on the cross. The crucified, resurrected, glorified Saviour longs to reign in your surrendered soul as King of kings and Lord of lords, "that the righteousness of the law might be fulfilled in us, who walk not after the flesh, but after the Spirit" (Romans 8:4)—not in the sweet bye and bye, but in the sweet here and now.

References

1. F. D. Nichol, *God's Challenge to Modern Apostasy* (Washington, D.C.: Review and Herald Publishing Assn., 1935), pp. 83-85.

2. Alexander Maclaren, *Exposition of Holy Scripture, St. Matthew* (New York: George H. Doran and Co.), p. 52.

3. *Ibid., St. Luke*, p. 339.

4. Nichol, p. 66.

5. Howard and Phyllis Rutledge, *In the Presence of Mine Enemies* (Old Tappan, New Jersey: Fleming H. Revell, 1973 and 1976), pp. 39-41, plus preface.

6. Arthur L. Bietz, *Exploring God's Answers* (Mountain View, Calif.: Pacific Press Publishing Assn., 1960), p. 17.

7. *Ibid.*, p. 4.

8. *Ibid.*, pp. 6, 7.

9. *Ibid.*, pp. 19-21.

10. Corrie ten Boom, *The Hiding Place* (London: Hodder and Stoughton, Ltd., 1972), pp. 220, 221.